Columbia, Conn. Congregational Church

The 150th Anniversary of the Organization of the
Congregational Church in Columbia

Conn., October 24th, 1866 - historical papers, addresses, with appendix

Columbia, Conn. Congregational Church

**The 150th Anniversary of the Organization of the Congregational Church in
Columbia**

Conn., October 24th, 1866 - historical papers, addresses, with appendix

ISBN/EAN: 9783337767334

Printed in Europe, USA, Canada, Australia, Japan

Cover: Foto ©Lupo / pixelio.de

More available books at **www.hansebooks.com**

THE

150TH ANNIVERSARY

OF THE

ORGANIZATION

OF THE

CONGREGATIONAL CHURCH

IN

COLUMBIA, CONN.,

OCTOBER 24th, 1866.

— — ·

HISTORICAL PAPERS, ADDRESSES,
WITH APPENDIX.

HARTFORD:
PRINTED BY CASE, LOCKWOOD & CO.,
1867.

26

THE

150TH ANNIVERSARY

OF THE

ORGANIZATION

OF THE

CONGREGATIONAL CHURCH

IN

COLUMBIA, CONN.,

OCTOBER 24th, 1866.

———•———

HISTORICAL PAPERS, ADDRESSES,
WITH APPENDIX.

HARTFORD:
PRINTED BY CASE, LOCKWOOD & CO.,
1867.

TABLE OF CONTENTS.

HISTORICAL DISCOURSE,

BY THE PASTOR, REV. FREDERICK D. AVERY.

It was just as the seventeenth century was flowing into the eighteenth that the inhabitants of Lebanon completed their town organization, gathered the first church and settled their first minister. Sixteen years after, in 1716, one hundred and fifty years ago, a second ecclesiastical society was constituted, which was known as Lebanon North Parish, or Lebanon Crank, until 1804, when Columbia became a town.

All efforts to ascertain the exact date of the organization of this *church* have been fruitless. The time would probably vary but little, if at all, from the formation of the ecclesiastical society. Taking the year 1716 as our stand-point, what would we find to be the religious aspect of the State? There were then but four counties in the State, Hartford, New Haven, New London and Fairfield. In all the State there were a few Episcopal societies, one Baptist, no Methodist. Of our own denomination, in what is now Hartford county, there were twelve churches, where there are now fifty-one; in what is now New Haven county, there were nine churches, where there are now forty-nine; in what is now New London county, there were eight churches, where there are now thirty-four; in what is now Fairfield county, there were eleven churches, where there are now thirty-six; in what is now Windham county, there were six churches, where there are now twenty-seven; in what is now Middlesex county, there were seven churches, where there are now twenty-six; in what is now Litchfield county, there were two churches, where

1

there are now forty-one; in what is now Tolland county, there were two churches besides our own, South Mansfield and South Coventry, where there are now twenty-two; in all fifty-seven churches in the State 150 years ago, where there are now 286 of our own denomination, 160 Methodist, 115 Baptist, and 130 Episcopal.

The early history of most of our old churches is very imperfectly known, for want of any thing that may properly be called Records; and in this misfortune this church shares largely. Of the first fifty years of the existence of this church, but a few meagre pages are to be found, as its own proper record at the time; and of the next seventy years we have scarcely more than the barest statistics of baptisms, admissions and deaths.

The first item that has been found indicating the actual existence of this church is the fact stated by Dr. Trumbull, that Mr. Samuel Smith was settled here in the year 1720. Mr. Smith was doubtless the first pastor. His ministry was of short duration, the parish granting his request to "lay down the pastoral office," December 24, 1724. He was a native of Glastenbury; was graduated at Yale College, in 1713, in a class of three, and was a tutor in the College. He died in 1725, only five years from the time of his settlement here, and twelve years after his graduation.

But one month elapsed and a call was extended to Mr. William Gager, who was ordained May 27, 1725. This second pastor continued his labors here nearly ten years, when the termination of his pastorate is thus declared by himself, September 4, 1735: "I, the subscriber, do by these presents desist the work of the ministry in the North Society in Lebanon, and release said people from all obligations they have made with me as to my support and maintenance for the future, and declare that I have no particular or special right to officiate as a minister among them." After leaving this people Mr. Gager preached one year in Eastbury. He was born in 1704, the son of Samuel and Rebecca Gager; was graduated at Yale College, in 1721, and died in May, 1739, aged thirty-three.

The third pastor was Rev. Eleazar Wheelock. Mr. Wheelock was born in Windham, in May, 1711, the only son of Deacon Ralph Wheelock. He was graduated at Yale College, in 1733, having for a class-mate Benjamin Pomeroy, who soon became his much-esteemed fellow-laborer as the pastor of the church in Hebron. He was licensed to preach the gospel by the New Haven East Association, in 1734. He received a call to settle here in February, 1735, and was ordained the first Wednesday in June following. The terms of his settlement are as follows: "Voted to give Mr. Wheelock that part of the minister's farm which they reserved in their agreement with Mr. Gager, which they suppose is something more than twenty acres, and two hundred pounds in bills of public credit, for a settlement, in case he settle in the work of the ministry among us. Also, voted to give Mr. Wheelock one hundred and forty pounds a year salary, to be paid in bills of public credit, or in provision at the following prices; viz. wheat at nine shillings per bushel, rye at seven, Indian corn at five, oats at two shillings and six pence, pork at six pence a pound, and beef at four; which are to be the standard by which his salary is to rise or fall proportionally as they in the general rise or fall among us."

Mr. Wheelock began his ministry here just at the time when commenced that marvelous work of grace in New England which is termed the "Great Awakening." He entered into this work from the very first, and became an earnest and efficient fellow-laborer with the Rev. Jonathan Edwards. Not a year had passed after his settlement before this parish was beginning to receive the 'fruits of his faithful and well-directed labors. Under date of 1736, stated by Jonathan Edwards to be in the Spring and Summer of that year, the historian brings this testimony: "The work also was very great at Lebanon Crank, a parish under the ministry of Rev. Mr. Wheelock, a pious young gentleman who had been then very lately ordained in that place." Of the real extent and duration of this revival here no certain statement can be made; nor do we know that there was any other period in his ministry that was so distinctly marked by the special power of the Holy Spirit.

Such success attended the preaching of Mr. Wheelock in that revival season, that he found himself, either by solicitation or from the impulse of his own earnest soul, drawn away from his own special field, to engage in like efforts with other churches and ministers, yet probably without neglecting his own flock. We find him in Enfield, July 8, 1741, listening to that memorable sermon of Edwards, entitled "Sinners in the hands of an angry God," from the text, "Their foot shall slide in due time;" and his report of that meeting to Dr. Trumbull, gives that historian this passage: "While the people in the neighboring towns were in great distress for their souls, the inhabitants of that town were very secure, loose and vain. A lecture had been appointed at Enfield, and the neighboring people, the night before, were so affected at the thoughtlessness of the inhabitants, and in such fear that God would, in his righteous judgment, pass them by, while the divine showers were falling all around them, as to be prostrate before him a considerable part of it, supplicating mercy for their souls. When the time appointed for the lecture came, a number of the neighboring ministers attended, and some from a distance. When they went into the meeting-house, the appearance of the assembly was thoughtless and vain. The people hardly conducted themselves with common decency. The Rev. Mr. Edwards, of Northampton, preached, and before the sermon was ended, the assembly appeared deeply impressed and bowed down, with an awful conviction of their sin and danger. There was such a breathing of distress, and weeping, that the preacher was obliged to speak to the people and desire silence, that he might be heard. This was the beginning of the same great and prevailing concern in that place, with which the colony in general was visited."

Three months later we find Mr. Wheelock journeying towards Boston, and he lets us trace his steps by his private journal, a few notes from which will serve to show us the spirit of the man, and the character of his labors.

"October 21, 1741. Rode to Voluntown. There is a great work in this town, but more of the footsteps of satan than in any place I have yet been in. At their conference in the evening I mentioned some of the devices of satan, which I apprehend they are in danger of, and heard the accounts of a number of new converts.

October 22. Rose this morning refreshed; found my soul stretching after God. Preached twice, with enlargement, by Mr. Smith's barn, to great assemblies. Many cried out; many stood trembling; the whole assembly very solemn and much affection; four or five converted.

24. About two miles from Providence, met Mr. Knight and another man, who came out to meet us. His first salutation was, 'God bless you, my dear brother.' Rev. Mr. Cotton came; invited me to preach.

25. Rode with Mr. Knight into town. Preached three sermons, 2 Cor. 13, 5; Mark 1, 2; Luke 10, ult.

30. Had a great sense of my own badness and unworthiness, of what a cursed heart I have. O Lord, let me see and know more of it. Rode to Norton. Preached to a full assembly; much affection and sobbing through the whole · assembly.

November 1. Went with brother Byram to Taunton; preached there. Appointed another meeting in the evening. A great work in the town. I was forced to break off my sermon before it was done, the outcry was so great.

November 2. Rode with a great number to Bridgewater. Preached to a full assembly, in Mr. Shaw's meeting-house.

3. Rode with a great number to Mr. Perkins' meeting-house. A very full assembly. So many wounded that I could not leave them. Therefore preached again to a full assembly.

6. Set out for Boston. Met by dear Mr. Prince and Mr. Bromfield, about eight miles from Boston. Came in to Mr. Bromfield's. Soon after my arrival, came the Hon. Josiah Willard, Secretary, Rev. Mr. Webb, and Mr. Cooper, and Major Sewal, to bid me welcome to Boston. At six o'clock preached for Mr. Webb, to a great assembly.

8. Went to Dr. Coleman's meeting; preached with considerable freedom. Dined with the Dr. Went with Mr. Rogers to Mr. Prince's. Preached to a full assembly. After

meeting was followed by a great throng of children, who importunately desired me to give them a word of exhortation in a private house, which I consented to do, though I designed to go and hear Mr. Prince, who, being by, desired that I would have it publicly, which I consented to.

9. Visited this morning by a great number of persons under soul trouble. Refused to preach because I designed to go out of town. Just as I was going, came Mr. Webb and told me the people were meeting together to hear another sermon. I consented to preach again. A scholar from Cambridge being present, who came to get me to go to Cambridge, hastened to Cambridge, and by a little after six a great part of the scholars had got to Boston. Preached to a very thronged assembly, many more than could get into the house, with very great freedom and enlargement. I believe the children of God were very much refreshed."

We see from these extracts how heartily Mr. Wheelock entered into this new revival-work, becoming indeed one of the chief leaders in it, and witnessing the same wonderful results of his labors abroad in other towns, that he had just before seen here at home. So constant were his efforts to bring sinners to Christ, that in one year "he preached a hundred more sermons than there are days in the year."

It might seem at times that he laid himself liable to the charge of being an enthusiast, as indulging in extravagancies and unwarranted hopes in respect to the character of his work. Yet he was actually so far from countenancing the extreme fanatics of his day, that we find one of those who were termed Separatists, dealing with him thus thoroughly:—"Yet all this,"—afflictions and losses that he had spoken of,—"never went so near to my soul as it does to hear and see the blessed work and ways of the glorious God, called errors and delusions of the devil. Pray, sir, let me deal plainly now, and don't be angry. Do you think you are out of danger of committing the unpardonable sin against the Holy Ghost? It would not surprise me much to hear that God had opened the flood-gates of his wrath, and let out the horrors of conscience on you, and many more of your party who deny the truth, so that you should die in as great despair as Judas or Spira did." So much for the attack on that side. But, on the other hand, many of the ministers of New England were very apprehensive of the result of this great movement, and some set themselves directly and strongly against it, cautioning their churches not to come under its influences. Members were suspended from communion "for going to hear Mr. Whitfield, Mr. Wheelock, Mr. Pomeroy, and other zealous preachers." Dr. Chauncey, of Boston, in a published work, represented Mr. Pomeroy and Mr. Wheelock as the principal instruments of the disorders and confusions in Connecticut. Between these two opposite pressures, it is quite likely that the pastor of Lebanon Crank pursued his even course, looking only to his Master for light and direction. There were men of rashness and of very folly in the methods which they adopted in that time of the Great Awakening, and with these Mr. Wheelock was sometimes indiscriminately classed. But one of the foremost of these men, Mr. James Davenport, came to see his sin and folly, and applied to Rev. Solomon Williams, of Lebanon, and Mr. Wheelock, to know what he should do; and, chiefly through the influence of these two ministers of Lebanon, he was led to a public confession and retraction.

Now would you know just what that preaching was which stirred the souls of your fathers and mothers of that olden time, and which wrought such commotion in many another parish, far and near? Listen then to the report by the historian, Dr. Trumbull, a native of Hebron, and who "lived sometime in the family of Dr. Wheelock." "The doctrines preached by those famous men," Pomeroy and Wheelock, "who were owned as the principal instruments of this extraordinary revival of God's work, were the doctrines of the reformation; the doctrine of original sin; of regeneration by the supernatural influences of the divine Spirit, and of the absolute necessity of it, that any man might bear good fruit, or ever be admitted into the kingdom of God; effectual calling; justification by faith wholly on account of the imputed righteousness of Jesus Christ; repentance toward God, and faith toward our Lord Jesus Christ; the perseverance of the saints; the indwelling influence of the Holy Spirit in them; and its divine consolations and joys."

Two of his sermons are particularly spoken of in the narrative of those revivals, as having been attended with marked results; one from the text, "What is the hope of the hypocrite though he hath gained, when God taketh away the soul?" showing "how far a man might go in religion, and after all be no more than a hypocrite," and then "the miserable end of the hypocrite;" the other from the text, "He that believeth and is baptized shall be saved, but he that believeth not shall be damned;" describing a "saving faith in Christ, giving many distinguishing marks of it, and finally insisting that all without exception, who would not believe, would most certainly be damned." Not many of his sermons were written in full; as his duties and cares became more pressing he employed only brief notes.

Mr. Wheelock received the degree of Doctor of Divinity from the University at Edinburg, June 29, 1767.

His labors in connection with Moor's Indian Charity School will be noticed in another place. It was in the interests of this enterprise that he deemed it best to sever his relation from this people, and move, with his pupils, into the wild lands of New Hampshire, where, in connection with the school, Dartmouth College was founded, and Dr. Wheelock became its first President.

In April, 1770, the ecclesiastical society concurred with the vote of the church to submit the matter of Dr. Wheelock's dismission to the decision of the western committee of the association of Windham county, with which association, this church, through its pastor, was then connected, and he was accordingly dismissed that year, having held the pastoral office thirty-five years. In August, he left for his new home in Hanover, New Hampshire; cut away the pine trees; built a log hut eighteen feet square; in three months after had a one story house for himself and family, and a two story house for his College; and in the next August a class of four young men was graduated. He presided over the College, preaching to the students and the people of the village, eight years. Having been seized with epilepsy he lingered three months, and, at the age of sixty-eight, died April 24, 1779, singing and longing, "Though I walk through the valley of the shadow of death, I will fear no evil." "I have a desire to depart and be with Christ."

Dr. Wheelock is described as "of middle stature and size, well proportioned, erect and dignified. His features were prominent, his eyes a light blue and animated. His complexion was fair, and the general expression of his countenance pleasing and handsome. His voice was remarkably full, harmonious and commanding. His movements while in the desk were natural and impressive, and his eloquence irresistible. His preaching and addresses were close and pungent, and yet winning beyond almost all comparison, so that his audience would be melted even into tears before they were aware of it."

He was first married in April, 1735, to Mrs. Sarah Maltby, widow of Capt. William Maltby, of New Haven, and daughter of Rev. John Davenport, of Stamford. She died in this place November 13, 1746, at the age of forty-three, and her grave is to be found near the center of the old cemetery. Her daughter Ruth was married to Rev. William Patten, of Hartford, and there are those still with us who remember Mrs. Patten in her old age, in Hartford, and who listened to her interested inquiries about Lebanon Crank. The second wife of Dr. Wheelock was Miss Mary Brinsmade, of Milford. They had five children; Mary, who married Bezaleel Woodward, first Professor of Mathematics in Dartmouth College; Abigail, who married Rev. Sylvanus Ripley, one of the first four graduates, and first Professor of Theology in the same institution; John, also of the first class, and successor of his father in the Presidency, nearly forty years; Col. Eleazer Wheelock and James Wheelock. Two sons by his first wife, both bearing his name, died in infancy, and are buried by the side of the mother.

The publications of Dr. Wheelock are, " A Narrative of the Indian Charity School at Lebanon," 1762; a Sermon at the

Ordination of Charles Jeffrey Smith, 1763; "Narratives" in
several numbers from 1763 to 1771; "Continuation of the
Narrative," 1773; A Sermon on "Liberty of Conscience, or
no king but Christ in the church," 1775. His Memoirs, by
Drs. McClure and Parish, were published in 1811.

In a scrap of Church Record which has been furnished from
Dr. Wheelock's old papers by Rev. William Allen, D. D., of
Northampton, who married his grand-daughter, we have the
following item : "At a meeting of the brethren of the church
of Christ in Lebanon North Parish, February 14, A. D.
1737–8, the church then voted that they would choose a com-
petent number of the most judicious, prudent and skillful of
the brethren of the church, and set them apart for, and commit to them, the management of all affairs in church government, in all ordinary cases, and appoint them to examine, try
and judge of the same in their name and behalf, under the
conduct of their minister or pastor, and to advise, assist and
help him in any matters wherein he shall desire or require
their help and assistance; and pursuant to this vote this
church made choice of these brethren, in the order following,
to represent them: Deacon John Newcomb, Deacon Joseph
Clark, Captain Ephraim Sprague, Mr. James Wright, Mr.
Nehemiah Clossen, Mr. Josiah Lyman, Mr. Thomas Woodward, Lieutenant Henry Woodward, Ensign John Daggett."
How long this Church Council, as it was called, was kept in
existence can not be determined, but since it appears to have
come into disfavor with some very soon, it is quite probable
that it was discontinued before the close of Dr. Wheelock's
pastorate.

A little more than two years passed and the fourth pastor
was settled, Rev. Thomas Brockway. Mr. Brockway was
born in Lyme, in the year 1744. He was graduated at Yale
College, in 1768.

In January, 1772, he received a call to settle over this
church and society. The terms of his settlement were as follows: "Voted to give Mr. Thomas Brockway two hundred
pounds settlement, one hundred to be paid at the end of the
first year, and fifty pounds at the end of each of the two fol-

lowing years. Also, to give him ninety pounds salary, and to
get him as many cords of wood yearly, at six shillings a cord,
as he desires, not exceeding thirty cords, to be reducted out
of the above ninety pounds."

He was ordained the 24th of June, 1772. The Wednesday
previous was observed as a day of fasting and prayer with
reference to the occasion. A person was chosen "in behalf
of the church and society to return thanks to the Reverend
Council for their kind assistance in ordaining Mr. Brockway."
The ministers invited on the Council were, Rev. Messrs. Solomon Williams, of Lebanon; Timothy Stone, of Goshen;
Joseph Huntington, of South Coventry; Benjamin Pomeroy,
of Hebron; Samuel Lockwood, of Andover; George Beck-
with and Stephen Johnson. The sermon was preached by
Rev. Samuel Clark, of Kensington, from 2 Cor. 4, 1, which,
in accordance with a vote of the society, was published.

The earliest Church Records, of any extent, are in the
hand-writing of Mr. Brockway, commencing with his settlement. When he began his ministry, the church consisted
of sixty-nine members; thirty-two males, and thirty-seven
females. He was with this people during the troublous times
of war, when the life of some of our churches, as well as of
many of our noble-hearted patriots, was put in jeopardy. He
was ready to share with his people in their pecuniary strug-
gles, proposing " to give in fifteen pounds a year till the enemy
withdrew, and ten pounds a year till the Continental debt be
paid." But this was not enough. As soon as the news of the
burning of New London reached this place, "he started off
with his long gun and deacons and parishioners to assist in
doing battle with the enemy."

The seasons of special religious interest during his ministry
will be noticed in his own words, taken from an account published near the close of his life, in April, 1803, in the Connecticut Evangelical Magazine. "Compared with other accounts, I have little to say, yet on the score of sovereign
grace, and the almighty power of the divine Spirit, in subdu-
ing the sinner, I have much to say. I can bear the same testimony with those that have labored in a larger field, that

with the Lord there is mercy, and with him is plenteous redemption. In the year 1781, it pleased God to revive his work among us; a special attention and uncommon seriousness seemed to prevail in all parts of the society; and the happy effects for many years were sensibly felt. At that season there were upwards of thirty added to the church. After that, there was nothing special took place, except in individual cases, for twenty years; during which period the spirit of vital religion was reduced to a very languid state. This will ever be the case without fresh anointings from the Spirit. Toward the latter end of March, in the year 1801, two or three pious people agreed to meet and pray for a revival of religion among us. This was soon discovered and others joined. The numbers increased weekly, and in the May and June following, our meetings became crowded, and the Spirit of God in the conviction of a number was evidently seen among us. A public lecture was appointed, in which I was favored with the kind assistance of my brethren in the ministry. Our conferences were attended three or four times in the week; but the most crowded, and that which discovered most of the power of the Spirit was on Thursday in the afternoon. During this period religion appeared not to be a secondary object, but the one thing needful. Sabbaths seemed too far distant, and the appointed seasons of conference were waited for with anticipated delight. The work, however, was far from being general among the people. There were some from almost every part of the society; and some families so peculiarly distinguished, that it might almost be said of them as of the favored house at which our Lord when in the flesh so often called, that they were all friends to Jesus. To the serious, contemplative mind, there was a striking display of the sovereign, discriminating grace of God. While one family was wholly occupied with the concerns of the soul, perhaps a few rods at the next door, nothing of it was to be seen; they were wholly unmoved, unless with a spirit of opposition. The work, in its early stage, took deep hold of professors. They seemed to awake as from sleep, and the prosperity of Zion was the object of their united prayers. Love to one another, and zeal for the cause animated them, with but few exceptions. The still small voice has characterized the work from the beginning, without any thing of an opposite nature."

One still remains with us who was a subject of that revival of 1801, and united with the church that year, whose wife,—also a subject and uniting with the church then,—has passed away during the present year. Thirty-five were added to the church as the fruits of that revival. The whole number admitted to the church during Mr. Brockway's ministry was 189, of whom twenty-nine were by letter.

Having been ill and not able to preach for a few weeks, he went to Lyme, his native place, for the benefit of his health, and there he died suddenly on the night of the fourth of July, 1807. His body was brought to Columbia, and on Monday the sixth, the funeral was attended by a large concourse of people. The sermon was preached by Rev. Zebulon Ely, of Lebanon, from Hebrews 13: 7, 8, "Remember them which have the rule over you, who have spoken unto you the word of God, whose faith follow, considering the end of their conversation, Jesus Christ, the same yesterday and to day and forever." And some there are still with us who do "remember," with reverence, with esteem and with affection, that holy man of God, who "ruled over" them so gently and with such a tender care for the flock, whose words were spoken as by the servant of God, and whose ministry was manifestly acceptable to the Great Head of the Church.

His pastorate was just the same number of years as Dr. Wheelock's, thirty-five. He died at the age of sixty-two, and you read upon his tomb-stone in yonder cemetery,—"As an husband, he was tender; as a father, affectionate; and as a friend, sincere. As a minister of Christ, he shunned not to declare all the counsel of God, and was wise in turning men to righteousness."

Mr. Brockway married Eunice Lathrop, of Norwich, December 18, 1772. They had thirteen children, three sons and ten daughters; two of whom, a son and daughter are buried by the side of the father. Mrs. Brockway died in 1823.

He published an epic poem, entitled "The Gospel Tragedy,"

in 1795; a sermon on "Virtue its own rewarder," in 1795; and one at the ordination of Bezaleel Pinneo, in Milford, October 26, 1796, from Colossians 1 : 26, 27.

Nearly four years elapsed before the fifth pastor was settled, Rev. Thomas Rich. Mr. Rich was born in Warren, Massachusetts, February 9, 1775, and was graduated at Dartmouth College, in 1799. He was ordained pastor of the church in Westbrook, June 13, 1804, from which church he was dismissed September 5, 1810. He was installed pastor of this church and society March 6, 1811. The sermon was preached by Rev. Salmon Cone, of Colchester.

During his ministry, in June, 1814, the church adopted a form of Covenant and Confession of Faith. Near the close of his ministry, in the year 1816, a season of revival was enjoyed, as the fruits of which forty-six were added to the church. He was dismissed June 13, 1817, having been pastor but six years. He afterwards preached in Sharon, Massachusetts, and in Salisbury, Massachusetts, and died in Amesbury, September, 1836, at the age of sixty-one.

The sixth pastor was Rev. William Burton. He was born in Washington, Vermont, and was graduated at Dartmouth College, in 1815. He was ordained here February 24, 1818; sermon by Rev. Chauncey Booth, of South Coventry. He preached but a few times, holding the pastoral office only sixteen months, and was dismissed June 23, 1819. From here he went to the southern states, but spent the chief part of his life preaching in Ohio, where he died in 1858.

The seventh pastor was Rev. David Dickinson. He was born in Conway, Massachusetts, July 22, 1770. He was first engaged in the medical profession for six years. After entering the ministry he was settled in Plainfield, New Hampshire, for eighteen years. He was installed here January 19, 1820. The churches invited on the Council were, Hebron, third church in Chatham, (now East Hampton,) Ellington, Exeter, South Coventry, and Andover. The sermon was preached by Rev. Amos Bassett, D. D., of Hebron; charge to the pastor, by Rev. Joel West, of Chatham; right hand of fellowship, by

Rev. Chauncey Booth, of South Coventry; and address to the people, by Rev. Diodate Brockway, of Ellington.

In the early part of Mr. Dickinson's ministry there were marked indications of the presence of the Holy Spirit, and his labors were blessed in many hopeful conversions, so that in the year 1821 there were added to the church by profession, twenty-three, and fifteen in each of the years 1823 and 1825. But in 1831, there was a more extensive and powerful work of divine grace; this church sharing largely in the blessing which was so widely experienced throughout the State. In that year forty-one were added to the church by profession. The whole number added during his ministry of seventeen years, was 123, of whom twenty united by letter. He was dismissed July 4, 1837. After his removal from this place he resumed the practice of medicine, and died in Mexico, N. Y., January 1, 1857, aged eighty-seven.

The eighth pastor, Rev. Charles Kittredge, was born in Newburyport, Massachusetts, in August, 1809, and was graduated at Dartmouth College, in 1834. He was ordained here March 27, 1839, after having supplied the pulpit nearly a year. The churches acting in the Council were, Ellington, South Coventry, North Coventry, Bolton, Andover, Hebron, North Mansfield, and Gilead. Rev. Bennett Tyler, D. D., of East Windsor, preached the sermon, from Isaiah 58, 1; charge to the pastor by Rev. George A. Calhoun, of North Coventry; right hand of fellowship by Rev. Alpha Miller, of Andover; and address to the people by Rev. William Ely, of North Mansfield.

In the latter part of the year 1839, the pastor proposed "an abridgement in the language of the Confession of Faith, and the addition of proof texts, and to have the same printed, together with the covenant and a catalogue of all the names of the members of the church, in pamphlet form, and one copy for each member;" which proposal, after due deliberation, was approved, and, on June 9th, 1840, our confession and covenant, as at present existing, were adopted.

Being unable to preach for a considerable time from impaired health, Mr. Kittredge asked the church to agree with him in calling a council for his dismission, to which request the church and society consented, and he was accordingly dismissed Feb. 16th, 1841, after a pastorate of only two years, in which time nine were added to the church. He afterwards preached, for a time, in West Greece, N. Y., in which place he now resides, without any pastoral charge.

The ninth pastor was Rev. James Wheelock Woodward, a descendant, in the fourth generation, of Dr. Wheelock. He was born in Hanover, New Hampshire, March 30, 1805, and was graduated at Dartmouth College, in 1826. For nine years he was pastor of the Presbyterian Church in Shrewsbury, New Jersey. After preaching here several months, he was installed March 23d, 1842. The churches comprising the council were, South Coventry, North Coventry, Andover, Gilead, East Stafford, Marlboro and Willimantic. The sermon, from II Cor., ii : 16, was preached by Rev. Jonathan Cogswell, D. D., of East Windsor; Charge to the pastor by Rev. Chauncey Booth, of South Coventry; Right Hand of Fellowship, by Rev. George H. Woodward, of East Stafford, brother of the candidate ; and Address to the people by Rev. Charles Nichols, of Gilead.

During the year previous to his settlement, his labors with this people were largely blessed, and 17 were added to the church near the close of the year. During his ministry 56 were received to the church. He was dismissed Oct. 12th, 1848, having been pastor nearly seven years.

After leaving this place he resided, for a time, in Flatbush, Long Island, and then in Albany, N. Y., where he was engaged in mercantile pursuits ; and again, for a few months, in Columbia; nearly all this time under treatment for that dread disease which was disfiguring his face and by which his life was terminated. His last two years were spent in Iowa, whither he went, as he said, " to die with his brother." He was, however, able to labor there happily and successfully, till near the close of his life, connected, most of the time, with the Congregational church in Irving. He died in Toledo, Iowa, at the house of his brother, Rev. George H. Woodward, Jan. 6th, 1864, aged 58. In his funeral sermon, preached by

Rev. Mr. Dodd, we have this passage: "How has grace abounded in all his comfort! always satisfied and thankful, he received his affliction as the wisely-directed allotment of a loving Father, chastening an erring child for his good. He felt, under all, that God is good when he afflicts as when he comforts. Though for a long time a great sufferer, he was never known to utter a word of complaint. While he had breath he praised his God. For years he had looked death in the face, and, though nature always shrinks from it as an enemy, through grace he had been enabled to see it disarmed of its sting, and to greet it with a smile, yea, with triumph. 'O, death where is thy sting? O, grave where is thy victory? Thanks be to God who giveth us the victory through our Lord Jesus Christ.' "

Mr. Woodward was married in 1834, to Miss Jane Tenbrook, of Shrewsbury, New Jersey. She died in Albany, New York, Dec. 6th, 1857.

The tenth and present pastor was ordained here, June 11, 1850. The sermon was preached by Rev. Abel McEwen, D. D., of New London; Charge to the pastor by Rev. George A. Calhoun, of North Coventry; Right Hand of Fellowship, by Rev. John Avery, of Exeter; and Address to the people by Rev. Samuel G. Willard, of Willimantic.

During the present pastorate the church has enjoyed three seasons of revival: in 1854, when 26 were added to the church; in 1858, when 20 were added to the church; and in 1865, giving an accession of 22. And besides these three, it is a most happy coincidence that we are observing this 150th anniversary just in the midst of a work of grace, so marvelous and so wide-spread in this town, reaching especially so many of the men and women in and past mid-life, that it seems as if we were indeed carried back to that mighty work of God, here in Lebanon Crank, in the first year of Dr. Wheelock's ministry. And just here would we desire to record our grateful sense of this great and undeserved favor of God, extended to us within the month past, in connection with the labors of Rev. John D. Potter.

The wife of the present pastor, Mrs. Julia S. Avery, daugh-

3

ter of Roswell and Phebe H. Smith, of New Haven, died here June 24th, 1855; and at the grave stands a fitting monument, erected by the ladies of the Parish,—a soothing token of their affectionate remembrance of one whose delight it was to share in the joys and sorrows and duties of the people whom she fondly loved.

In the latter part of the year 1860, a new catalogue and manual was printed for the use of the church. The present list of members contains 130 names, 47 males and 83 females.*

THE DEACONS OF THE CHURCH.

Of some of these scarcely more can here be noted than the bare names. No date of election can be positively ascertained until the beginning of the present century. Previous to that time we take the year in which they are first called deacons in the society records, as very near the time of their election. The first deacons mentioned are Samuel Wright and John Newcomb, and these persons undoubtedly officiated from the first.

Deacon Samuel Wright, died April 18, 1734, aged 61.

Deacon John Newcomb was the son of Simeon and Deborah Newcomb, and was born in Edgarton, Mass., about the year 1688. He moved from here to Cornwallis, Nova Scotia, where he died Feb. 22, 1765.

Deacon Joseph Clark is mentioned as holding the office as early as 1735. His tombstone bears this testimony: " Capt. Joseph Clark Esq., a man who was faithful in his private and public life; used the office of deacon well, endured his last sickness with patience, and died in hope of a blessed immortality, Sept. 10, 1769, in the 78th year of his age."

Deacon Eliakim Tupper, is spoken of in the year 1741, but how long he held the office, or when he died, is not ascertained.

Deacon James Wright is also mentioned as early as the year 1745.

*To this number add 39 received into the church in Jan. 1867, of whom 3 by letter.

Deacon Josiah Lyman held the office from about 1750 till his death, Feb. 6, 1760, at the age of 70.

Deacon Thomas Lyman served about the same time, and we have this record on his tombstone : " He was a man of great experience in the christian religion. Few in our world have enjoyed a more constant communion with Heaven, or, at intervals, had greater discoveries of divine things. His life was zealous and exemplary, his death was peaceful and triumphant. He did great honor to religion while he lived, but greater when he died. · In his last moments were seen the power of the divine life and the most convincing proof of the truth of the christian religion." He died Aug. 13, 1785, in the 80th year of his age.

Deacon Israel Woodward united with this church in 1736, and was performing the duties of the office as early as 1752. He died July 30, 1797, in the 90th year of his age. We have this inscription at his grave : " He was eminent for his piety towards God and usefulness to the world, and came to his grave like a shock of corn fully ripe. The memory of the just is blessed."

Deacon James Pinneo, born in 1708, held the office as early as 1755. He died April 16, 1789, aged 80 ; and his tombstone tells us :
> "The sweet remembrance of the just,
> Shall flourish when they sleep in dust."

Deacon Preserved Wright was holding the office at the time of Dr. Wheelock's removal, and accompanied him to Hanover, N. H.

Deacon Jabez Kingsbury is spoken of as early as 1768, but no further record is found of him.

Deacon Samuel Dunham united with the church in 1741. On his tombstone is written : " A man of real worth in private and public character, his usefulness in society was such that he might fitly be called a blessing in his day. He professed hearty friendship to the cause of Christ, which both his life and his death witnessed to be genuine. In the lively hope of a blessed immortality, he departed this life Dec. 9, 1779, in the 62d year of his age."

Deacon Daniel Dunham, son of Deacon Samuel Dunham, united with the church in 1769. He removed from town, and where and when he died has not been ascertained.

Deacon Wadsworth Brewster is remembered by two or three of the oldest members of the church, as fulfilling the duties of the office in the first days of their communing with this church. He died May 30, 1812, at the age of 75, and at his grave we read : " Mark the perfect man, and behold the upright; for the end of that man is peace."

Deacon James Pinneo, son of Deacon James and Priscilla Pinneo, was born April 5, 1734 ; united with this church in 1793 ; and died June 14, 1824, at the full age of 90.

Deacon Samuel Barstow, was born in Exeter, April 8, 1760. When he was about ten years of age, his father moved into this Parish. At the age of seventeen he yielded his heart to Christ after a protracted struggle, in which he was made to see the fearful guilt of his strong rebellion against God. He did not, however, unite with the church till Sept., 1781. He was chosen deacon in 1801. The characteristic feature of his spirit and life would quite truly be expressed by that scripture, " not slothful in business, fervent in spirit, serving the Lord." He was, ever ready to introduce and carry on religious conversation. In seasons of religious interest in neighboring towns he would find it his delight to be present with his whole soul, sharing in and helping on the good work. " In 1801 he was one of three brethren who commenced a weekly prayer meeting in his own district on Thursday evening. They longed for a revival of religion, and they determined to seek it in the appointed way. They began to inquire of the Lord for it. And while they were yet speaking, the Lord heard and answered them. The meetings filled up, christians awoke to prayerful efforts, and sinners inquired, ' what shall we do?' " Thus began that powerful work of grace in 1801–2. So too in 1816, he was very active in originating those meetings for prayer which resulted in another blessed revival. And even when he had passed his fourscore years, " he wished to be a fellow-helper to the truth, and consented to act as one of a committee to go from house to house and converse and pray with families. Just before his death, he said, "I am willing to stay just as long, and suffer just as much pain, as may please the Lord. But I long to go. I feel that for every brother on earth, I have fifteen in heaven, and I long to be with them. I love them, but I love the Saviour more. Precious, precious Saviour." He died Feb. 27, 1846, aged 86. A sketch of his life was published in pamphlet form, and was made one of the tracts of the American Tract Society.

Deacon Daniel Lord united with this church by letter in the year 1800. He was chosen to the office in 1801. He removed from this town to Bolton where he died in 1834.

Deacon Henry Bliss was chosen to the office in 1810, and died May 27, 1815, at the age of 73.

Deacon Benjamin Lyman, son of Benjamin and Elizabeth Lyman, united with this church Oct. 18, 1809. He was chosen deacon in 1813, and having obtained help of God, he remains with us until this day. He had anticipated this Anniversary with very great interest, hoping he might have strength to be present, but the hand of his Heavenly Father is upon him in sickness and infirmities, and he is only awaiting a happier day than this.

Deacon Sylvester Manley united with this church Oct. 18, 1809, and was chosen deacon in 1815. He removed to Pennsylvania where he died in 1833.

Deacon Silas Holbrook, son of John and Sarah Holbrook, united with this church in 1814. He was chosen to the office in 1831. A man of great simplicity of character, and of devout, humble spirit, earnest and importunate in prayer, his memory is cherished with esteem by the whole community. He died Feb. 19, 1861, aged 79.

Deacon Lorenzo W. Dewey, son of Eleazar (the sole remnant of the revival of 1801,) and Lydia Dewey, united with this church in 1823. He was chosen deacon July 8, 1843, and is still performing the duties of the office.

Deacon Chester W. Lyman, son of Chester and Sophia Lyman, united with this church in 1823, and was chosen deacon April 30, 1858, which office he still holds.

THE SABBATH SCHOOL.

This school was first organized in May, 1820, chiefly through the agency of Rev. Alfred Wright. Deacon Benjamin Lyman was the first superintendent, which position he continued to hold for fourteen years. The first lesson given to the school was the first chapter of John, and each scholar was to repeat as many verses as could be remembered. The scholars in those classes of 1820, have mostly passed away in death, a few remain to compare those beginnings with the school of the present day, which numbers about 150. For 35 years the school was discontinued through the winter, but the last 10 or 12 years show that it has an unbroken life. It has had a part in benevolent contributions, annually for 9 years previous to May, 1865 ; since which time by weekly collections. The Fortieth Anniversary of the school was observed in 1860.

Such is a cursory glance at the history of this church, extending over a period of 150 years. It has had its trial scenes, but not so severe as many of the early planted churches. It has preserved, nearly complete, its original territory, the sole occupant. It has not been subjected to those unhappy vicissitudes which are incident to a fluctuating population. Generations have come up, one after another, adopting, quite generally, the same form of christian doctrine and mode of worship, thereby preserving unimpaired the strength and numbers of the church ; and this, doubtless, is to be attributed, in a great measure, under God, to the thorough doctrinal inculcation and long continued labors of its two early pastors.

Here also have been experienced, from time to time, refreshing seasons from the presence of the Lord, enkindling anew the faith and the zeal of the church, and gathering spiritual harvests from each successive generation.

In view of these untold blessings, with what gratitude and praise to the Great Head of the Church should we remember all this way. God hath given you the goodly heritage. He established it here and has preserved it through more than "the third and fourth generation," that it may be a blessing to you of to-day. Here, on this day of commemoration, give God the praise, and forget never, all these his benefits.

Remember also, with grateful affection, those fathers and mothers in Israel, who, at whatever point in all this way, be it earlier or later, have passed on before you to their Heavenly Father's rest. They acted and planned with reference to those who should come after. For *you* they labored, for *you* they prayed. Be yours the grateful heart, the affectionate remembrance and the just appreciation of their self-denying exertions in behalf of this beloved Zion.

Here also take up a due sense of your own responsibility. These blessings have descended to you by vigilance and faithfulness on the part of your fathers. Just in the same way must these blessings pass down to your children and your children's children. The inheritance, handed down so far in its integrity, is now in your hands, and yours is the responsibility of transmitting it, unimpaired, to those who come after you. Be mindful then of this solemn and weighty responsibility ; be faithful to your priceless trust, that at some distant Anniversary day, fifty and a hundred years hence, it may be among the highest sources of gratulation, that here, even in *your* day, the people of God were found seeking the Lord and Zion was made to prosper.

TRIBUTE TO THE MEMORY OF REV. THOMAS BROCKWAY, ONE OF THE PASTORS OF THE CHURCH.

By Doct. O. B. Lyman, Hartford.

One spot dear to memory let us turn now to view,
The scenes of the past it will call up anew;
'Tis that spot where once stood the house for God's praise,
Where worshiped the fathers in earlier days.
The house in its structure was ancient and plain,
Its pews did no carpets or cushions contain;
No soft seated sofa its pulpit to grace,
No costly chandelier to light up the place;
No glowing hot furnace to displace the cold,
Unknown were such things to the churches of old.
As an aid to the speaker's laborious tongue,
O'er his head a broad sounding canopy hung;
And perched on its top was the form of a dove,
An olive branch bearing the emblem of love.
There first in the pulpit we, hoary heads, saw
An advocate stand for the truth of God's law,
And heard him proclaim the Gospel of Peace,
To the mourner a solace; to the captive, release.
There first too we heard from the "church going bell,"
The saddening deep tones of a funeral knell;
Or its call on the Sabbath for such as inclined,
To go up to the temple to seek food for the mind.
As onward time sped in its work of decay,
There arose a desire for modern display;
And at length 't was resolved a new structure to raise,
That would better compare with the taste of our days;
But the site of the former most lonely is left,
And of all that was sacred seems sadly bereft.

Mark yonder old church-yard where all is at rest,
How calmly it lies there declined to the west;
This sacred spot enter with reverent tread,
'Tis a place of reposit—a rest for the dead;
Our fathers sleep there awaiting their time,
To arise and put on immortality's prime;

And affection has reared many monuments there,
Breathed many a sigh, and shed many a tear,
O'er the graves of its kindred where silent they lie,
While angels their spirits have beeked up on high.
How often we've wandered those lone graves among,
And thought of that numerous celestial bright throng,
Of spirits immortal that peacefully roam,
Through the elysian fields of the blest spirit home!
Did sometimes the question then seem to arise,
"Do these spirits roam far beyond the fair skies?
Or do they draw near by an influx of soul,
Our thoughts and affections for good to control?"

Mark there 'mid the graves of his people appears,
The tombstone of BROCKWAY, grown mossy with years;
Long, long has he lain there beneath the cold sod,
Yes, almost forgotten, that servant of God.
Now could he to earth from the spirit-land come,
And visit the spot where of old was his home,
View the change that appears on the old village green,
Where he walked in his day with dignified mien,
Find the temple removed where he anciently stood,
And pictured the cross stained with innocent blood,
Old structures demolished and new ones upthrown,
Familiar old faces and kindred all gone,—
On the prospect how strangely his spirit would gaze,
While the change it contrasted with primitive days!

4

HISTORICAL SKETCH.

By John S. Yeomans.

THE second or new Ecclesiastical Society, as it was then sometimes called, was incorporated by the General Assembly of the Colony, at their May session in 1716. It is supposed that the Society immediately acted in the matter of procuring a minister, but we have no record evidence preserved for the next eight years.

The first entry on our records is December 24th, 1724, when "Mr. Samuel Smith desired the Parish that he might lay down his Pastoral office to which they consented by vote." From that date to the present time we have a continuous, unbroken record of the transactions of the Society. The territorial limits of the Society, as defined at that time, are the same as the present boundaries of the town; with the exception of the triangular tract, set off to Andover, on the formation of that Society, about the year 1748, and which contained at that time about twenty-four tax-payers, as appears by rate bills extant. The main portion of the territory was included in what is known as Clark and Dewey's purchase, and Joseph Clark and Benony Clark, two of the sons of William Clark, the Proprietor, were among the first settlers, and were the leading men of the Parish.

The first acts of the Parish show that they were actuated by the same spirit that sent our Pilgrim Fathers to this then wild and rock-bound shore,—"Freedom to worship God,"—consequently the Church and the School House claimed their earliest attention; and we will first endeavor to trace their foot-prints in this direction.

MEETING HOUSES.

THE first Meeting House was raised probably some time during the summer of 1724.

Where the Rev. Samuel Smith held his meetings we have no means of knowing, but probably at the house of Joseph Clark.

A Parish meeting was held January 27th, 1725, at which meeting they " Voted to give the Rev. William Gager a call to settle with us in the work of the Ministry;" they also " voted to remove the meeting to the house of Benony Clark."

At a Parish meeting held December 15th, 1725, they " voted to John Mory twelve shillings for sweeping the Meeting House." This is the first record we have in regard to a Meeting House. It was probably covered and the floor laid and occupied during the summer for worship on the Sabbath.

At a Parish meeting December 14th, 1726, " voted to make provision for laying the gallery floors, and for making the stairs and finishing the coving and building the breast work of the gallery, and for making steps for the three doors, and appointed Henry Woodward, Lieutenant Martin, and Josiah Lyman, to manage the affair; also, voted to Deacon Wright one pound for sweeping the Meeting House."

December 26th, 1728, " voted to procure boards to seal the Meeting House, and for the pews, and slit work for the galleries and pews, and all other stuff needful for the work."

December 4th, 1730, " voted to do something towards finishing the Meeting House."

November 3d, 1731, " voted to finish the seats and plaster the walls of the Meeting House; Captain Sprague, Lieutenant Woodward, and Sarjeant Daggit to see the work executed."

During the season of 1732, it seems that the Parish had so far completed their first Meeting House that at a special meeting held January 10, 1733, " they voted to Seat the Meeting House."

As this is a practice that has almost universally gone out of use, I give, as a curiosity, the entire record of this meeting.

" Made choice of John Sims, Joseph Clark, and Thomas Woodward to be a committee to seat the Meeting House. Voted that no man shall be brought lower than he was seated before.

Voted that the seaters should reckon one, and but one head to each list.

Voted to seat the Meeting House by the last Rate or List.

Voted to vallew one year's age to two shillings in the rate.

Voted that the pews next to the great door shall be vallewed next to the first or highest pews, and those by the stairs equal to the second seat ; the fore seat in the front to be equal to the second seat in the body of the Meeting House, and the fore seat in the side gallery, to be equal to the sixth seat.

At the same time they made choice of Deacon Wright, Captain Sprague and Sarjeant Lyman to be a committee to seat the seaters."

At the same time they " voted that Samuel Woodward, Israel Woodward, William Simes, Noah Dewey, Samuel Wright and Preserved Wright, shall have liberty to build themselves a seat or seats, a pew or pews, for them and their families, in the front gallery, behind those seats that are already built; to be built at their own charge ; and also be debarred from any other seat in the Meeting House ; they to have all the room that is behind the seats that are now built."

With the gradation of the pews, the definite property qualifications as determined by the last list by which they were to be seated, a committee of their own choice to seat them, and a sub-committee to seat the seaters, it would seem that they might worship in their new house with quiet minds and contented spirits. February 8th, 1733, less than a month from the time of the appointment of the seating committee, another meeting is called, and it is " voted that the pew by the great door in the Meeting House, shall be reconed equal to the fore seat and corner pew ; and also voted to accept of what the seating committee had done." Whether the pew by the great door was not sufficiently dignified, or those who were assigned to it were degraded, we have no means of knowing. At any rate it seems that a vote of the Society was needed to give characteristic dignity, either to the pew or people; and we need not smile at this act of our ancestors, for similar developments of human nature exist to-day.

The size of this Meeting House is not known. It was probably about forty or fifty feet in length and breadth, as the votes show that there were galleries on three sides, wide enough to have pews built back of the seats, which could not be done in a house of less dimensions.

It was probably a rude building at best, as is usually the case with pioneer settlers, for in November, 1733, they " voted to repair the windows, both wood and glass, and also to make new steps; also to give liberty to Joseph Loomis, John Sims, and Benony Loomis, to build themselves a pew over the women's stairs, not hurting the stairway nor the window." This last vote was probably not carried out, for in November, 1740, " the Parish Committee were authorized to grant liberty to Nathaniel White, Jun'r, John Payne, with sundry others to build a seat or pew over the women's stairs, as they think proper ; also voted to fill up the broad alley with seats and to take down the coving of the Meeting House ;" and in 1744, " to fill up the aisles at the east end of the Meeting House."

At a Parish meeting, November 22d, 1744, probably about twenty years only from the time the first house was raised, the proposition to build a new one was brought before the Parish, and they voted in the negative ; also, at the same time " voted not to repair or make addition to the old one." But the Great Awakening of 1741 had passed over New England. The new Pastor, Rev. Mr. Wheelock, was active in it : his people had shared largely in its blessing, and the church accommodations were insufficient for the thronging multitude which each returning Sabbath brought to its courts.

Consequently at their annual meeting the next year, Nov. 21st, 1745, they " voted to make some provision for building a new Meeting House and to make repairs upon the old one for present comfort." The location of this house is learned from the location of the second which was determined by a committee appointed by the Legislature in 1747, to " ascertain and fix a place to set a Meeting House upon, among us."

This committee reported that they had stuck a stake about ten rods south of the present Meeting House on the common, —the sills of the house to enclose the stake. This Meeting House, as many of us will remember, stood in front of the present dwelling house of Mr. John Armstrong, consequently the first Meeting House stood about where the school house now stands and most probably on the same ground.

In 1747 "The Society voted to build a new Meeting House, 64 feet in length and 46 feet in width and 26 feet in height from the top of the sill to the underside of the plate. Also voted to get the timber, hew, and frame and raise it, cover the roof and board the outside and provide timber, either pine or ceder, for the window frames, by the first day of Dec. 1748, and also voted a tax of two shillings upon the pound towards defraying the charges of the Meeting House, also a tax of 13 pence on the pound for Parish charges, and appointed Captain Joseph Clark, Ensign Nathaniel Cushman, and Lieutenant Benajah Bill, a committee to carry on the work of building, so far as they have agreed to do it."

In August, 1748, " Voted to clapboard the south side and the ends with Ceder, and the back side with Chestnut, and to do it this fall." 1 record this fact for the purpose of showing the care bestowed by the Parish in the selection of the building material of this house. These clapboards were still on the house when it was taken down in 1832, eighty-four years from the time they were put on ; and it was thought by many better to remodel and repair the old house than to build new, because the outside covering was so good ; as many of us well recollect. Oct. 5th, 1749, "voted to improve the old Meeting House toward finishing the new one, either by sale or any other way ;" and in Sept. 1751, " voted to finish the house within two years."

"Also appointed Joseph Clark, Benajah Bill and Nathaniel Cushman to carry on the work."

The probability is that the Sabbath worship was held in the new house at this time, as a vote was passed to seat the Meeting House.

In December, 1753, " voted to Collour the Meeting House sky collour and also to pave round it with round stone or flatt and to make such alterations in seating as the Com'y think proper."

In Dec. 5th, 1754, a Parish meeting was held, at which time they " voted to settle with the meeting house committee at this meeting. The accounts were cast up and, errors excepted, amounted to £4458 1s. 4d." ($14,860.00.) This certainly shows a good degree of energy and perseverance in a small parish with but 170 tax payers, as appears by old town and Parish rate Bills of that day.

In the year 1792, a Steeple was erected and a Bell procured by subscribers at a cost of $150.00. The vote of the Parish is as follows: " Voted, to give liberty to the subscribers for building a Steeple, to erect one and annex it to the west end of the Meeting House, and furnish it with a Bell, and if so erected and furnished with a Bell, the society will receive it as theirs and afterwards keep it in repair."

From the time the Steeple was erected, Mr. David Huntington was Bell ringer, till his death in 1828; a period of 36 years; and no man was ever more attached to Idol than was he to the Bell. At 12 o'clock at noon and 9 o'clock P. M. year in and year out, the tones of this Bell moved by his arm would be heard by the people. And if, (as was often the case,) some urchin on mischief bent, could find his way into the Meeting House and commence ringing the Bell, no night was so dark, no storm so pelting, but that the old man would hasten to the Meeting House, and rest not till every window and door was examined and secured. Wo! to the wight who should chance to be caught. But the agile feet of youth were usually too fleet, and seldom were they caught. Yet I apprehend that more than one who hears me to-day, would, if that faithful, honest and good old man were to rise from his grave and appear in our midst, feel like asking his forgiveness for the annoyance which, in the hilarity and thoughtlessness of youth, they had caused him.

Of the present Meeting House I propose to say but little, as all the people of middle age are acquainted with the facts

1775. He was ordained pastor in Sandown, New Hampshire, Dec. 27, 1780. He was dismissed April 30, 1788, and in Nov. following was installed over the Presbyterian church in Hanover Center, New Hampshire. This church, being but a remnant of that from which the majority had been taken by the former pastor, "his ministry there was beset by trials. He was, however, universally esteemed as a devoted and excellent christian minister." He was again dismissed in 1795; and, after a brief ministry in Craftsbury, he died in that town Jan. 7, 1807, at the age of 59.

Daniel Crocker was graduated at Yale College in 1782, and was licensed by the New Haven West Association, in 1788. He was settled in Redding in Oct., 1809, where he remained till Oct., 1824. He was again settled in New Fairfield in Oct., 1827, and died in March, 1831.

Walter Harris was born in 1761, the son of Nathaniel and Grace Harris. He served three years in the war of the Revolution, his only brother falling a sacrifice in that struggle, and was honorably discharged when less than nineteen years old. He removed to Lebanon, New Hampshire, where he came under the influence of a powerful revival of religion, and gaining satisfactory evidence of his conversion, he devoted himself to the work of the ministry. He was graduated at Dartmouth College, in 1787. Having studied Theology with Dr. Emmons, he was ordained pastor of a church which he was instrumental in organizing in Dunbarton, New Hampshire, Aug. 26, 1789. He received the degree of Doctor of Divinity from Dartmouth College, in 1826.

As a preacher he was said to be "mighty in the scriptures. He uttered himself with a deep solemnity that showed that he never lost sight of his own final account. He chose out acceptable words, but they were charged with an energy which it was not easy to resist." One of his hearers once said, "every sermon of his is a broad-axe, cutting away every refuge of lies, and laying prostrate every thing that exalteth itself against the knowledge of God." He received many young men as Theological students, who ever after held him in the highest estimation, as a man and as an instructor.

Towards the close of his active duties as pastor, we have this testimony concerning him from one who is remembered by some here to-day, as a school-master in Hop River District, Rev. Dr. Barstow, of Keene, New Hampshire ; his words are, "I was struck in those days with his deep humility and unwavering confidence in God, with his comprehensive views of the christian system, and the facility with which he could put to silence the ignorances of foolish men. I could not but feel that he was a master in Israel, and that it was good to sit at his feet and listen to his instruction." And this same witness recalls these words spoken to him by Dr. Harris when at Saratoga for the benefit of his health :—"I told my people the last Sabbath, that I had done ; that I had cared for them for more than forty years, without leaving them unsupplied for many Sabbaths, and that now they must take care of themselves ; that I hoped they would hold fast the doctrines which I preached, for I verily believed they were the truth of God, and I would willingly risk my own soul upon them. The people were somewhat affected, and I too was affected with the thought that I must meet them at the bar of God. I warned them to meet me as the disciples of Christ, that I might not be a swift witness against them." After these forty years' labors he was not able to continue the active duties of the ministry, yet he remained with his people till his death, Dec. 25, 1843, at the age of 82. Fifteen of his sermons were published, also an address before the Pastoral Convention of New Hampshire.

Ezra Woodworth was born in 1765. He was graduated at Dartmouth College in 1788 ; was ordained pastor of the first church in Winsted, Jan. 2, 1792 ; was dismissed in 1799, and died in 1836, aged 71.

Joel West, son of Samuel and Sarah West, was born March 12, 1766. He was graduated at Dartmouth College in 1789, and ordained pastor of the third church in Chatham, (now East Hampton,) in Oct., 1792. He remained the esteemed and faithful pastor of that church till his death, in Nov., 1826, at the age of 60.

Bezaleel Pinneo, son of Deacon James and Jerusha Pinneo,

was born July 28, 1769. He was graduated at Dartmouth College in 1791 ; studied Theology with Dr. Smalley ; was licensed by the Hartford South Association in Oct., 1793, and was ordained pastor of the first church in Milford, Oct. 26, 1796. While pursuing his labors as pastor, he acted, for a time, as instructor of students of Theology, among whom was the distinguished Evangelist, Rev. Dr. Nettleton, remembered by some who are here to-day, as preaching for a few Sabbaths before the settlement of Mr. Kittredge. Mr. Pinneo remained in the active duties of the pastoral office forty-three years, very widely known and respected, as excellent in judgment and earnestly devoted to his work. Bearing the infirmities of age for nearly ten years, he died among his people Sept. 18, 1849, aged 80.

Diodate Brockway, second son and third child of Rev. Thomas and Eunice Brockway, was born Dec. 29, 1776. He was graduated at Yale College in 1797, united with this church in Sept., 1798, studied Theology with Rev. Elijah Parsons of East Haddam, was licensed by the Middlesex Association, Oct. 3, 1798, and was ordained pastor of the church in Ellington, Sept. 19, 1799. He retained the pastoral office fifty years, though by reason of his infirmities he had the assistance of colleagues the last eighteen years. He was a Fellow of Yale College from 1827 till his death. He died Jan. 27, 1849, aged 72. *He published a sermon, preached at the funeral of Deacon Gurdon Elsworth, 1803 ; another at the dedication of the Meeting House in Ellington in 1806 ; a sermon before the Missionary Society of Connecticut ; an Election sermon in 1818, and a New Year's sermon in 1828.

Jacob Allen, son of Timothy and Mary Allen, was born Aug. 18, 1781. While studying with Rev. E. T. Woodruff, in North Coventry, he hopefully became a subject of divine grace, and turned his thoughts towards the ministry. He was graduated at Dartmouth College in 1811, studied Theology with Dr. Burton of Thetford, Vt., was licensed by Orange Association, and ordained pastor at Tunbridge, Vt., in Oct., 1813. He was dismissed in 1820 and installed in Eastbury in July, 1822. Being dismissed in 1835, he was installed over the church of Voluntown and Sterling Oct. 11, 1837, where he remained until Nov. 15, 1849, when he was dismissed and supplied the church in Long Society in Preston for one year, after which he returned to his last charge, supplying the pulpit there until he died, March 13, 1856, at the age of 75.

He is described, in a sermon preached at his funeral by Rev. Henry Robinson, as "a sound and able Theologian, an earnest and instructive preacher; eminently gifted in prayer, a faithful and devoted pastor, a wise and safe counsellor; given to hospitality, remarkable for humility, most affectionate and exemplary in domestic relations, interested in benevolent operations." He was a frequent contributor to periodicals and newspapers, both secular and religious. He preached the sermon at the dedication of this house.

Alfred Wright, son of Jeriah and Temperance Wright, was born March 1, 1788. He is spoken of while a child as being of a sober, thoughtful turn of mind, and possessed of an uncommonly studious disposition. His father, with limited means, and with a family of eleven children, could not gratify his thirst for knowledge. He repeatedly expressed his desire to obtain an education and become a minister of the gospel, even before he was satisfied of his conversion. With feeble health, and in the face of formidable obstacles, he pursued his course of preparatory studies at the Colchester Academy, and joined the sophomore class in Williams College, where he was graduated in 1812. Thus far, not regarding himself as a Christian, his mind was directed to the study of medicine, and by his occasional reading of medical books, he gained an amount of information that qualified him to render essential medical service in the field of his future labors. But a few months before his graduation he was reckoned among the fruits of a revival in College, and from that time he entertained the design of entering the ministry, and, if it was the clear indication of providence, of engaging in a foreign mission. While connected with the Andover Theological Seminary, he was also engaged as instructor in Phillips Academy. Being appointed tutor in Williams College, he entered upon the duties of that office in October, 1814. Visiting home in the winter of 1815, he was prostrated with sickness, and the disease was of such a nature that but little hope was entertained of restoration to an active and useful life. He turned towards the south for his health, and was able to take charge of a Female Academy in Raleigh, North Carolina. In the winter of 1818, he was licensed to preach, and on the 17th of December, 1819, he was ordained as an Evangelist, in the Circular Church, Charleston, by the Congregational Association of South Carolina. At the same time was ordained Jonas King, the now veteran missionary, lately from his great life-work in Athens. Mr. Wright turns from a call to settle in Charleston to the Choctaws in Elliot, Georgia, and thus he enters upon the life of missionary toil to which he had looked forward, though in a field different from that which he had anticipated. Ten years he spent with the Choctaws before their removal beyond the Mississippi, having the care of a church, conducting schools, preparing elementary school books in the native language, and in time of sickness being in constant demand for medical attention and advice. On the removal of the Indians to their present territory in 1831, some of the missionaries retired from the field, but Mr. Wright was among those who, in compliance with the earnest entreaties of the Indians, and in obedience to a sense of duty, accompanied them to their new home. He entered his new field of labor in September, 1832, and selected a site which he called Wheelock, in memory of the former pastor of his native town. A church was organized on the second Sabbath in December, 1832, with thirty-seven members. And here, as his central point, do we find him for the next twenty years, toiling on in patience and hope, and often with the most cheering success; all the while "with a feeble frame, never without pain, unable to walk more than a few rods, or raise with his hands more than a few pounds weight."

But the great labor of his life was the translation of the Holy Scriptures into the Choctaw language. Upon this the full energies of his mind and body were bent. It was his earnest wish to finish translating the Bible, but this was too great a work for one man, with all the difficulties which embarrassed him : at the same time superintending the schools, and having the care of two or three churches. By diligent application he carried the work of translation through the New Testament, and from Genesis to Job, in the Old Testament. His motto, in his own words, was, " Labor, incessant labor on earth, and rest, eternal rest in heaven." Nor was his labor in vain. Sometimes forty and sixty or seventy in a year would be reckoned among the converts within his particular field of labor.

The great secret of his success was that "he walked with God." His spirit of devotion and of Christian solicitude for the spiritual welfare of others is breathed forth, especially in his early letters home, when, as a son and brother, he faithfully and affectionately and personally exhorted and entreated his friends all to make Christ their Saviour, and to engage with their full energies in his service. He always retained an affectionate remembrance of his native place, and of this church, inquiring after its welfare, rejoicing with it in its seasons of refreshing, and bearing it on his prayers before the throne of grace. He died March 31, 1853, aged sixty-five, peacefully committing all to his Saviour, saying, " Good is the will of the Lord concerning me." He had no more to do but to lie down and die. He was in his master's work, and ready for Heaven every day. When the word came to go up higher, he just ceased his labors and obeyed.

> " Servant of God, well done,
> Rest from thy loved employ,
> The battle fought, the victory won,
> Enter thy Master's joy."

James D. Chapman was born in May, 1799, was graduated at Yale College, in 1826, preached one year in Prospect, and was settled over the church in Wolcott, in 1833. He was dismissed in 1840, and afterwards settled in Cummington, Mass., where he died December 19, 1854, aged fifty-five.

Daniel Hunt, son of Daniel and Submit Hunt, was graduated at Amherst College, in 1828, studied theology at Andover Seminary, and was ordained pastor of the church in Pomfret,

April 8, 1835, where he still resides, although dismissed from his charge, and from feeble health no longer able to fulfill the duties of the ministry. He has published a historical sermon ; also, valuable historical papers in connection with the 150th anniversary of the church in Pomfret, which was duly commemorated October 26th, 1865.

Amasa Dewey, son of Asahel and Lucina Dewey, was born March 12, 1804, united with this church in 1821, and was graduated at Yale College, in 1832. He studied theology at East Windsor Seminary, was licensed by the New Haven East Association, in 1838, and ordained pastor in Petersham, Mass., January 11, 1837, where he died January 5, 1840, at the age of thirty-five. A small volume of practical sermons, from his pen, was published after his death.

Ansel Dewey, son of Asahel and Lucina Dewey, was born August 9, 1809, and united with this church in 1831. He studied theology at East Windsor Seminary, was licensed by the Hartford North Association, December 14th, 1836, but, before assuming any pastoral charge, died August 6th, 1838, aged twenty-nine.

Charles Little, son of Samuel and Jerusha Little, was graduated at Yale College, in 1844, a classmate of the present pastor. He studied theology at New Haven, united with this church in 1847, and was ordained, in this house, September 1st, 1847 ; sermon by Rev. Joel Hawes, D. D., of Hartford. He entered upon the missionary work in the year 1848, and labored faithfully and successfully at several stations in the Madura Mission, until 1859, when, by reason of impaired health, he returned to this country, relinquishing the foreign field. Having, in good measure, regained his health, he was installed pastor of the church in Cheshire, January 1st, 1862. Since leaving Cheshire, he has been engaged with the first church in Woodbury, where he is now laboring.

HISTORICAL PAPERS.

By John S. Yeomans.

The first vote of the Parish in regard to Education, is January 6th, 1732, when they made choice of "Captain Ephraim Sprague, Nehemiah Closson and Deacon Wright, to be a school committee to receive our part of the country money, and to lay it out at their discretion, for the instruction of Children in the Parish." From this date forward regularly at the annual meetings a like committee was appointed till 1798, when the organization of school societies took the place of towns and ecclesiastical societies, in our school system. That we may better understand this matter, perhaps a brief digest of our school laws during the period of our 150 years of ecclesiastical life may be appropriate.

From 1701 to 1800 the law of the Colony may be summed up as follows:

1st. An obligation on every parent and guardian of children, " not to suffer any child or apprentice to grow up in their families, unable to read the holy word of God and the good laws of the Colony, under penalty for each offence.

2d. A tax of forty shillings on every £1,000 of the lists of estates, collected with the annual State tax, and payable proportionately to those towns only which should keep schools according to law.

3d. A common school in every town of seventy families or over, to be kept through the year, and in towns of less than seventy families, at least six months in the year.

4th. A Grammar School in each of the four counties at their county seats, to fit youth for College; which Grammar Schools must be free.

5th. A Collegiate School towards which the General Court made an annual appropriation of £120.

6th. Provision for the religious instruction of the Indians.

In May, 1717, the obligation resting upon towns in regard to education was extended to parishes under the same provisions, and we as a parish took charge of our schools.

In 1686 the Assembly made a grant to the plantations of Hartford and Windsor, of the north-west portion of the State comprising the present towns of Norwalk, Goshen, Canaan, Cornwall, Kent, Salisbury, Sharon, Torrington, Barkhamsted, Colebrook, Harwinton, Hartland, Winchester and New Hartford, to preserve them from the grasp of Sir Edmund Andros, who acting for James the first, claimed all the unappropriated lands of the State as belonging to the King.

But though the Charter Oak which preserved our Colonial Charter lives only in history, yet the Charter which it held, remains, and, encased in the wood which protected it, hangs gracefully, in the office of the Secretary of the State in Hartford. So also did Sir Edmund fail to get possession of the unappropriated lands of the Colony. After the danger from Andros was passed, the Governor claimed the lands as fully as though no grant had been made. Hartford and Windsor however, on the strength of the grant by the Assembly, and the settlements commenced under it, determined to resist the claim and oppose the legislature. Great disturbances ensued.

Finally, however, in 1726, forty years after the grant, the dispute was settled, and the legislature resolved that the lands in controversy should be divided between the Colony and the claiming towns of Hartford and Windsor.

The Colony was to have the western townships, viz., Norfolk, Goshen, Canaan, Cornwall, Kent, Salisbury and Sharon ; and Hartford and Windsor, the eastern, viz., Torrington, Barkhamsted, Colebrook, Harwinton, Hartland, Winchester and New Hartford.

The legislature appointed a committee to view the townships belonging to the Colony, who reported in May, 1733, as their opinion that the legislature should grant all the moneys which shall arise from the sale of the seven townships, to the towns of this Colony which are now settled, to be divided to them in proportion to the grand lists of said towns, and to be secured and improved forever, to the use of the schools kept in the several towns, according to law; which report was accepted, and a committee appointed to make sale of the lands.

From this sale came the local fund of about 300 dollars now held by this town, the interest of which has annually been applied in accordance with the law. In the Revised Statutes published in 1750, it was enacted that the money distributed to towns and societies, and called " Local School funds," remain a perpetual fund for the support of schools, and for any application of the interest to other purposes, the principal was to be paid back into the treasury of the Colony, and the town or society was to lose the benefit thereof afterwards, and such is the law to-day in regard to said fund.

While on the subject of the law, I may as well say that Societies or Parishes for religious purposes were first established in 1700; authorized to choose a clerk in 1716; a committee in 1717; a collector in 1721; a moderator in 1726, and a treasurer in 1764, and in 1717, the right to tax for school purposes as well as for the support of the ministry. Under this provision this Society had charge of the schools in the Parish till 1795, when the moneys arising from the sale of the western lands belonging to this State, were ordered to be invested and called the " School Fund," and remain a perpetual fund, " the interest of which shall be inviolably appropriated to the support and encouragement of the public or common schools throughout the State, for the equal benefit of all the people thereof."

In 1798, the management of schools passed from towns and ecclesiastical societies as such to school societies especially constituted for this purpose.

The Parish, from its organization, had taxed themselves every year for the support of the ministry, for schools and other purposes, until 1818, when the adoption of the present State Constitution gave religious liberty and equality of civil rights to all religious sects; since which time the means for the support of the gospel have been raised, sometimes by tax, sometimes by sale of slips and voluntary contribution.

In 1739, the Parish " voted to raise by tax, £50 (167 dollars) to be added to the " country money," to keep a school of two school masters for the three winter months, for writing and reading, and to be removed from place to place for the best advantage of the parish in general. And the rest of the money to be improved in hiring school dames, to teach children to read the rest of the year, as shall best suit the parish in general, and appointed a committee to see that schools be kept as above expressed."

I infer from these votes that there were no school houses in the parish at this date, but the schools were kept in private houses.

In 1744, the Parish, after voting to keep a school according to law, and appointing Rev. Mr. Wheelock, Deacon John Newcomb, and Mr. Josiah Finney, to see that it be done, also "voted that the neighborhood adjacent to the meeting house have liberty to build a school house on the commons near the meeting house; also that the neighborhood adjacent to Thomas Porter have liberty to build a school house near said Thomas Porter's house.

Also voted that the school house which Mr. Josiah Finney has set on the highway should stand in that place." The school house in the center district was probably not built by the district at that time, but in stead was erected the house for the "Indian Charity School," which is the present house of the center district, remodeled, and which passed into the hands of the district, I can not find when, or how, by any record extant.

In 1768, a committee of three persons out of the parish, were chosen to determine, divide and set off the school districts in the parish.

In their report they say: "Whereas, there hath been three districts, Middle, North and South, we are of opinion that they remain the same, although at present the middle district, being fewer in number, and less able to maintain a school, recommend that the north part be reckoned with the north district, and the south part with the south district, they having right at any time when they shall be able and inclined, to build a school house, and set up a school within their limits." Until 1773, but three persons had been appointed school committee, probably one in each district. In that year five were appointed, one in each district that then existed, probably ; to wit, " Henchman Bennet, Rufus Collins, Jabez Wright, Nathaniel White, and Lieut. James Pineo."

The next year six persons were appointed, the center district probably having resumed their place as a district.

The six districts remained as they were then till the formation of school societies in 1788, and remain still the same, with the addition of the south-west, the territory of which till 1816 was an unbroken forest, known as " Wells' Woods."

MUSIC.

At a Parish meeting February 21st, 1737, " voted to sing in the public worship according to the rule by which they sing in the old Society in Lebanon." " Also made choice of Eleazer Hutchinson to set the psalm in the congregation."

" Also made choice of Joseph Clark to set the psalm when Mr. Hutchinson is absent or can not."

With this arrangement they rested satisfied, so far as the records show, till 1774, when on the 28th of June, a meeting of the Parish was held and it was put to vote, " whether they would sing by rule in the assembly ; voted in the affirmative."

Also " voted that the choristers should set such tunes as they think proper."

This was doubtless a special meeting on the subject, as no other business was transacted or votes passed.

In 1791, at their annual meeting, voted " a tax of one-half penny on the pound to encourage singing, and to be applied for that purpose only ; and chose Enos Gary and Asahel Allen collectors of the singing tax."

In 1794, voted " that they desire Messrs. Samuel Bliss, Seth Collins, Ambrose Collins and Samuel West Jr., to take turns in leading the singing on Sundays."

In 1798, " James Pineo, Esq., John Newcomb, Seth Collins, Samuel Bliss and Consider Little, were appointed a committee to promote singing."

In 1806, voted " to request Samuel West, Jr., Benjamin Lyman, Dan Porter, and William Hunt to lead in singing for the year ensuing."

In 1813, " Messrs. S. Barstow, S. Manley, G. Lincoln, J. Richardson, E. Woodworth and N. Tanner, were appointed a committee to get subscriptions to revive the singing, and to hire a teacher if they get enough subscribed."

In 1819, " voted that Deacon Benjamin Lyman be requested to revive the singing in this Society."

This is the last date, I believe, in which the Society, as such, have acted in regard to singing.

The choir have usually circulated their own subscriptions, hired their own teachers, and chosen their own choristers.

And although a body of persons whose sole object and aim should be to make harmony in singing the songs of Zion in the sanctuary of the Lord, it can not be denied, but that sometimes elements of discord have found their way into the choir, musically speaking, as well as otherwise.

MISCELLANEOUS.

A reference to a few miscellaneous transactions of the Society, and I will tire your patience no farther with the prosy recital of Parish votes.

In 1750, the Parish voted " to allow Samuel Woodward and his brethren liberty to build them a Sabbath day house, some where near the old Meeting House, where the parish committee think proper."

In 1751, voted " to empower the parish committee to erect a sign post, at some convenient place on the south side of the Meeting House, and that proper notifications set on said post for parish meetings shall be accounted legal." When the Society became a town they, (the town,) by agreement with the Society, made it their sign post, and when the present house was erected, the town concurred in removing the sign post to the place where it now stands.

In 1755, the following preamble and votes were passed :

" *Whereas*, Mr. Joshua More, of Mansfield, has given a lot of land in the 2nd Society in Lebanon, for the foundation, use and support of a Charity School, forever to be known and called by the name of the Charity School in Lebanon, founded by Joshua More for the education of Indians, &c." At a legal meeting of said Society, Nov. 18, 1755, it was voted "that if said school shall be set up, that in order to their regular, comfortable and orderly attendance upon the public worship of God, the boys in said school shall have for their use, the pew in the gallery, over the west stairs in the Meeting House ; and further provision suitable for them in said Meeting House shall be made if there shall be occasion."

In 1761, "voted to allow Mr. Wheelock's Indian girls liberty to sit in the hind seat on the women's side below."

The first half century of our Parish life closed in the year 1766. This had been a very prosperous period with both the Church and the Society. The Society had built their large and commodious house of worship, which, as tradition tells us, was filled to overflowing ; the whole mass of the population, at that period, being in the habit of attending church regularly and constantly on the Sabbath. They had emerged from that trial state which is incidental to the settlement of a new country ; they had been prospered in temporal things, and had built for themselves those stately dwelling houses, of which some of us, who are half century men, have a vivid recollection, but of which very few now remain.

An event transpired at this time which though not a part of our Society history, proper, yet so connected with it, that a committee was appointed the next year which reported a manifesto which occupies four pages of our Society records, being adopted and placed there by vote of the Society.*

It was the sending to England, by Mr. Wheelock, of Rev. Nathaniel Whitaker, then pastor of the church in Chelsea, (now Norwich Landing,) and Samson Occum, an Indian preacher, both of whom had been educated in this place by Dr. Wheelock.†

The next half century, closing with the year 1816, was generally a period of trial with the Society, not on account of divisions among themselves, but on account of the troubles growing out of the conflict with the "Mother Country," which finally culminated in the Seven years war of the Revolution, which gave us Independence and National life, but which destroyed for a time our commerce, which before had been so profitable, sweeping away many an estate which was

---

*See Note A, Appendix.   †See Note B, Appendix.

supposed to be ample, and leaving heavy debts upon individuals, as well as the nation, from which during this half century they were hardly able to recover. They managed, however, to keep their light burning on this altar; yet many were burdened with pecuniary embarrassments, and heavy liens upon the lands they cultivated, and to add still to this, just at the close of this period, came a second war with England to add its weight of trouble to their burdens. The culmination seemed to be in our century year 1816, which is the memorable year of the present century, as the cold season. It was chronicled at the close of the year that in New England there were frosts during every month in the year. On the 16th day of June, a heavy frost killed all the corn, so that hardly a farmer in town raised a bushel of sound corn.

With the year 1817, commenced the last half century of our Parish life, and with it came a year of fulness to the garners of the husbandmen, giving to them courage and hope, and a happy presage of the prosperity and thrift which has rested upon us as a people for the last fifty years.

It has been emphatically a period of prosperity to this community, and to the whole country. The improvements in science, literature, and arts, are unparalleled in any former time. New motive powers have been discovered, by which transporting vehicles of giant dimensions, and fitted up with all the luxury of palatial dwellings, are rushed over land and sea with a velocity that outstrips the wind, so that the distance between places at one extreme and the other of our great country, is almost annihilated.

And yet again, we have set up poles and hung upon them iron wires, tying together all the principal towns and villages, all over our extended country; and over these, through the agency of a subtle element called electricity, we send messages all over the land, as quick as the "lightning that lighteneth out of one part under heaven shineth unto the other part under heaven," so that New Orleans, with which it took months to communicate at the commencement of our last half century of Society life, now has its important news and price-current published in the daily papers of all our New England cities, on the day the event transpires.

And within the past year we have had laid down amid the coral and dark depths of ocean one of these wires, and are now holding communication with the "mother country," on the other side of the Atlantic. But I must suppress these thoughts, which seem to come over me unbidden, while I speak of our prosperity as a Society for the last half century and then close.

In 1816, the dwelling houses were mostly in a dilapidated condition, weather-worn and mostly unpainted; such as were painted were a dingy red. I can recall to mind but two in the town at that time that were painted white. All were warmed by fires in the large old fashioned fire places of, the olden time. There were no stoves in town; no warming of the meeting house whatever; not more than two or three houses with a carpet upon any of its floors; no one horse wagons, the people riding to church on horseback, very often the man with his wife or daughter on a pillion behind him.

In two or three instances families living remote came in heavy lumbering hacks, as they were then called, and which was considered as rather an aristocratic way of going to church.

I think I am safe in saying that the great mass of the people in town at that time were more or less in debt. Money did not circulate freely, and the business transactions were mostly on credit; the farmers getting their groceries of the merchant, and in the fall paying the account in beef, pork, and the surplus produce of their farms, feeling satisfied if they got money enough to pay taxes.

To-day, as compared with fifty years ago, we are abundantly blessed. The most of our dwellings have put off their brown, and are painted white; are comfortably furnished, warmed, and carpeted.

The majority have probably been built new or essentially remodeled. The lands are much better cultivated, and the products of our crops per acre are much greater than formerly. Our farmers have, in the main, paid off their debts, and many of them have a small surplus invested in stocks, or at interest. And though we have no rich man in town, in the common

7

acceptation of the term, yet the great mass of our people have at their hands enough to satisfy all reasonable wants. The evidence of rural improvement and taste is seen about most of our dwellings, and I believe a good degree of comfort and hospitality reigns within. The church in which we are now convened, in its plain simplicity, and devoid as it is of architectural beauty, as compared with the old one in which in my boyhood on many a winter's Sabbath day I have sat listening to the creaking of its timbers, the rattling of window panes, and the howling of winter winds, and waiting, not so much "upon the Lord in his sanctuary," as for the *lastly* of the minister's sermon, which foreshadowed a speedy deliverance from the biting cold within its walls. I say as compared with that, the present house seems to me to be about all we can reasonably desire. But of the thousand thoughts which come up in this connection I can not now speak.

Now in conclusion, let me say to the youth and children present, a few, and but a few of whom will be present when fifty years hence, the people of this Parish shall meet to celebrate the two hundredth anniversary of this Church and Society, as I trust they will, may you so live that you may not only give to the Lord a good account of your stewardship, but pass over to your children the trusts which we commit to you.

And now I charge you that you guard well the interests of this Church and Society. See to it that you keep the fire burning brightly on this altar; that these seats with each returning Sabbath are filled with devout worshipers; that this desk is filled by a devout and faithful Pastor. Be kind to the aged and bear with their infirmities as they totter down the declivity of life, and when you shall grow old may you be able to commit all these sacred trusts reposed in you to *your* children, untarnished, unimpaired.

And finally, may we all so live as to be accounted faithful stewards, and on "the other side Jordan" be permitted to meet in reunion in that " city that hath no need of the sun, neither of the moon, to shine in it, for the glory of God doth lighten it, and the Lamb is the light thereof."

ADDRESS,

BY REV. CHARLES LITTLE, OF WOODBURY.

Mr. President and Friends:

IT is with peculiar satisfaction that I avail myself of this privilege of addressing you. Returning to this home of my childhood, for many years a wanderer, though not a fugitive, over the face of the earth, to share in the festivities and solemnities of this occasion, I have been in common with you all, most deeply interested.

Permit me, sir, to congratulate yourself and the committee of arrangements, on the success of this anniversary. I desire to express my personal obligations to your pastor and others who have labored so successfully to interest and instruct us.

This old town of Columbia, small as it is, and apart from the whirl of business, has an honorable history. Her sons and daughters need not be ashamed of their birth-place. Some may tell us that " it is a good place from which to emigrate," but I have felt to-day that it is a good place in which to live and to die; that here one may fill up a useful life and exert influences which shall magnify his own and others' happiness throughout eternity.

Thronging memories come up to me of scenes in my childhood and early youth, upon which I love to dwell.

I remember those gorgeous sunsets witnessed from my father's house, and those severe thunder storms which stirred my youthful blood. It seems to me that I have never beheld any since quite so grand and delightful.

I recall with pleasure those various schools which I attended, common and select, Sabbath and singing. In respect to physical and temporal blessings I have never enjoyed myself so well as then. Those were happy days. But my companions in those scenes—where are they? Some of them are here, strong in manhood's prime, but the larger part are absent; many scattered over the land; many in their graves. Looking over this congregation I recognize a few of them, and others who were then in active life, now bent and white by reason of age, but the majority here are strangers.

One hundred and fifty years ago! What mighty changes have occurred during this brief period! Then the population of this State was probably less than fifty thousand, only a few hundreds more than are now living in the city of New Haven. The settlements were confined to the vicinity of the Sound and rivers, leaving the large part of the State an unbroken forest. The far West was then this side the present city of Utica.

Contrast the changes in the manner of living and in the modes of conveyance; mark the progress made in the subjugation of the wilderness, in the growth of cities and villages, in new machinery and manufactures, in increased facilities for business.

Within this time how has the world itself been enlarged and at the same time compressed together! Its vast territories, then unknown, have been opened up to our knowledge; its population has increased from about seven hundred and fifty millions to twelve hundred millions. Yet the ends of the earth were never so near to each other as now. We can travel round the globe in a few weeks,—we can exchange morning and evening salutations with our brothers across the ocean.

This occasion inspires within us thoughts and feelings too precious to be forgotten. We feel our obligation to our forefathers and foremothers. To them under God we owe this rich inheritance. Their wisdom, toils and prayers obtained for us this history, so honorable and hallowed. How shall we repay them? We may do it by honoring their memories, not only to-day but continually. We may do it by training our children to excel ourselves in all that makes the useful citizen, the efficient Christian.

We owe a large debt of gratitude to God for what he has wrought in our town. For this church, for the institutions of the gospel planted and preserved here, for revivals in years long past, for refreshings in recent times, for the present powerful work of grace, we are unspeakably indebted to Him.

Oh what fervency of grateful love, what activity of sanctified powers should be presented to Him who has thus wonderfully proved His willingness to bless. From henceforth let us have a stronger confidence in God that He will fulfill His promises, that He will work out the redemption of the world.

We are here taught our duty to work for God. Had not the generations whose deeds have been rehearsed in our hearing, labored for God, these blessings would not have been ours. Let us emulate their example; let our consecration as much exceed theirs as our privileges are greater than theirs.

Be encouraged, ye who have been long enrolled in Christ's army. Fear not, faint not. Fight on, fight manfully. Victory, honor, trophies many, and crowns eternal shall be yours.

Ye who have recently entered the service of Christ, whether days many or few remain, be faithful. Important is the work before you. Be faithful and your Master shall reward you with the plaudit—"Well done."

To the youth and children present, one word. We wish you, we expect you to become better men, better women, more useful citizens, more efficient Christians than your fathers and mothers have been. Your privileges are great, your opportunities are vast, your obligations are infinite. I charge you, be true to yourselves, be true to your God.

This is indeed a joyous occasion. It is delightful, this review of the past; this revival of former friendships; this social intercourse; this interchange of feeling; this hallowed communion with each other, and perchance with the spirits of many whose bodies rest in these cemeteries; but I must not dwell.

I look forward with confident hope to another re-union more blessed than this. There will be families in unbroken succession. There, from many parts of this land, from the red men of the forest, from the idolators of India, will be gathered many witnesses to the fidelity and power of this church.

Here we meet for a few hours and part to see each other no more in the flesh, but there our re-union will continue forever. There through cycles endless, we shall progress in the service, the love, the joy of God our Father, and of His Son our Saviour. May we all be there.

MOOR'S INDIAN CHARITY SCHOOL,

ITS SCHOOLMASTERS AND MISSIONARIES.

BY THE PASTOR.

AMONG the earliest missionary efforts in the country, long before the organization of the "American Board," must be noted the Indian Missionary School of Rev. Eleazar Wheelock, pastor of the church in Lebanon Crank, now Columbia. This enterprise deserves notice, particularly because of its early date and worthy intention. It, however, was not without some good fruit in its work among the Indian tribes, and is to be regarded as of peculiar interest and importance, as leading to the establishment of Dartmouth College.

In December, 1743, Mr. Wheelock received into his family school, Samson Occom, a Mohegan Indian, whose successful course of education led to the project of training Indian youth to become missionaries to the various accessible tribes. For the encouragement of this enterprise Mr. Joshua Moor, of Mansfield, gave a lot of land near the center of the parish. A school house was soon built, situated on the corner east of the Hartford, and south of the Willimantic road, opposite which, at the north, was Dr. Wheelock's house. The school was sustained, and the missionaries sent out from it were supported by appropriations from the legislatures of Connecticut and Massachusetts, by funds received from England to the amount of seven thousand pounds sterling, of which the King gave two hundred pounds, by funds of the Scotch Society for Propagating Christian Knowledge, and by other church and individual contributions.[*]

This project assumed such importance at the time that it received the hearty commendation of the following neighboring ministers, in a paper drawn up and signed by them, under date of "Chelsea in Norwich, July 10, 1762:"

---

[*] See Note B, Appendix.

Ebenezer Rosseter, pastor of the first church in Stonington.

Joseph Fish,	"	second "	"
Nathaniel Whitaker,	"		" Chelsea.
Benjamin Pomeroy,	"	first "	Hebron.
Elijah Lathrop,	"		" Gilead.
Nathaniel Eells,	"	a "	Stonington.
Mather Byles,	"	first "	New London.
Jonathan Barber,	"		" Groton.

Matthew Graves, missionary at New London.

Peter Powers, pastor of the church in Newent.

Daniel Kirkland, formerly pastor at Newent.

Asher Rosseter,	"	first church,	Preston.
Jabez Wright,	"	fourth "	Norwich.
David Jewett,	"	second "	New London.
Benjamin Throop,	"	a "	Norwich.
Samuel Mosely,	"	a "	Windham.
Stephen White,	"	a "	"
Richard Salter,	"	a "	Mansfield.
Timothy Allen,	"		" Ashford.
Ephraim Little,	"	first "	Colchester.
Hobart Estabrook,	"	a "	East Haddam.
Joseph Fowler,	"	" "	"
Benjamin Boardman,	"	fourth "	Middletown.
John Norton,	"	sixth "	"
Benjamin Dunning,	"	a "	Marlborough.

Besides this we have another paper of commendation, dated New Jersey, September 5, 1765, which, among many other words, bears this testimony:

" We whose names are hereunto subscribed do certify that we have had frequent opportunities of being well-informed of an Indian Charity School which was some years ago instituted in the Colony of Connecticut, and which, by the continued smiles of Heaven, hath remarkably succeeded under the care of the Rev. and worthy Mr. Eleazar Wheelock, &c.

Thomas Gage, Commander-in-chief of His Majesty's forces in America.

Francis Bernard, Governor of Massachusetts.

Benjamin Wentworth, Governor of New Hampshire.

William Franklin, Governor of New Jersey.

John Penn, Lieutenant Governor of Pennsylvania.

Thomas Fitch, Governor of Connecticut.

Cadwallader Colden, Lieutenant Governor of New York.

William Allen, Chief Justice of Pennsylvania.

Frederick Smith, Chief Justice of New Jersey.

Theodore Atkinson, Chief Justice Superior Court of New Hampshire.

Mark H. Wentworth, of His Majesty's Council in New Hampshire.

Daniel Warner, Judge of the Common Pleas in New Hampshire.

William Smith, Justice of Superior Court in New York.

Peter Levins, of his Majesty's Council in New Hampshire.

Samuel Woodruff, of his Majesty's Council in New Jersey.

Joseph Shippen, Secretary of Pennsylvania.

Theodore Atkinson, Jr., Secretary of New Hampshire.

W. P. Smith, Mayor of Elizabethtown, New Jersey.

Andrew Elliott, Collector in New York.

Henry Sherbourn, of the House of Representatives, New Hampshire.

John Goff, of the House of Representatives, New Hampshire.

William Smith, Jr., Lawyer in New York.

John Morin Scott, Lawyer in New York.

William Livingston, Lawyer in New York.

Henry Wisner, of the General Assembly in New York.

Eleazar Miller, of the General Assembly in New York.

John Redman, M. D., in Philadelphia.

John Morgan, M. D., in Philadelphia.

William Farquhar, Benjamin Y. Prime, James Smith, Physicians in New York.

Abraham Gardner, Col. in East Hampton.

Samuel Smith, Daniel Roberdeau, Merchants in Philadelphia.

P. V. B. Livingston, James Jauncey, David Shaw, Garr. Rapalje, John Smith, John Provost, John Vender Spiegel, William M'Adams, Laurence Read, Dirk Brinkerhoff, Garrat Noel, Merchants in New York.

Samuel Seabury, Thomas B. Chandler, D. D., Jacob Duche, Ministers and Missionaries of the Church of England, by order of the Presbytery of New York, James Caldwell, Clerk.

John Ewing, Charles Beatty, Richard Treat, John Strain, Ministers in Pennsylvania.

Samuel Finley, D. D., President of the College in N. J.

Lambertus De Ronde, Archibald Laidlie, Joan Ritzema, John Albert Weygand, Ministers of the Protestant Dutch Church in New York.

Thomas Jackson, Preacher of the gospel in New York.

Ebenezer Prime, Thomas Lewis, Silvanus White, James Brown, Samuel Buel, Ministers on Long Island.

Naphtali Daggett, S. T. P. in Yale College, Connecticut.

Jonathan Parsons, Minister in Newbury, Massachusetts.

Samuel Haven, Minister in Portsmouth, New Hampshire.

John Rogers, Joseph Treat, Ministers in New York.

The number of scholars ranged from fifteen to twenty-five, about one half Indians, the others being English youth devoted chiefly to the work of missions among the Indians. The principal tribes from which these Indian pupils came, and the method of conducting this enterprise will be fairly indicated by this record of a hundred years ago:

"March 12, 1765, the Board of Correspondents met to examine Mr. Titus Smith and Mr. Theophilus Chamberlain, of their qualification for missionaries, and approved them. And also examined and approved David Fowler, a Montauk Indian, and Joseph Woolley and Hezekiah Calvin, Delawares, for schoolmasters among the Indians. They also examined Jacob Fowler, a Montauk, Moses, Johannes, Abraham Primus, Abraham Secundus, and Peter, Mohawks, and approved them as well accomplished for schoolmasters, excepting their want of age, and therefore appointed them to serve in the capacity of ushers, under the direction and conduct of the missionaries."

Of those who were actually sent out as missionaries only a brief mention can here be made.

Samson Occom, born in 1723, was ordained by the Suffolk

8

Presbytery on Long Island, and labored among the Montauk Indians, the Oneidas, and several other tribes, until 1766, when he was sent to England, in company with Rev. Mr. Whitaker, to solicit aid for the school. Being the first Indian preacher that had ever visited that country, he quickly enlisted an interest in himself personally, and in his mission, which proved a very successful one. He gained the reputation, both at home and abroad, of being an able and impressive preacher. His labors among the Indians were attended with the blessing of God. He preached a sermon on the execution of an Indian at New Haven, in 1772, which was published. He wrote an account of the Montauk Indians, which is still in manuscript. He was the author of that familiar and stirring hymn, "Awaked by Sinai's awful sound." In the latter part of his life he labored at various places in the vicinity of Albany, and a barn is still pointed out in the Mohawk valley by those who heard him preach in it seventy-five or eighty years ago. He died in New Stockbridge, New York, July 14, 1792, in the sixty-ninth year of his age.

It does not appear that any other Indian youth from Dr. Wheelock's school became ordained missionaries. Many, however, were sent out as schoolmasters, and schools which promised well for a time were gathered in several of the tribes of the Six Nations. Here is a peep into one of these schools which we take through the eyes of one of the missionaries: "I am every day diverted and pleased with a view of Moses and his school, as I can sit in my study and see him and all his scholars at any time, the school house being nothing but an open barrack; and I am much pleased to see eight, ten or twelve, and sometimes more scholars sitting round their bark table, some reading, some writing, and others a studying, and all engaged, to appearance, with as much seriousness and attention as you will see in almost any worshiping assembly, and Moses at the head of them with the gravity of a divine of fifty or threescore."

And here are a few words from one of these schoolmasters, David Fowler, of the Montauk tribe, writing to Dr. Wheelock from his station among the Oneidas:

"Kanavaroharc [Canajoharie,] June 15, 1765.

Honored and Rev. Sir,

This is the twelfth day since I began to keep this school, and I have put eight of my scholars into the third page of their spelling book; some have got almost down to the bottom of said page. I never saw children exceed these in learning. The number of my scholars are twenty-six, when they are all present, but it is difficult to keep them together. They are often roving about from place to place to get something to live upon. I am also teaching a singing school. They take great pleasure in learning to sing. We can already carry three parts of several tunes. My friends are always looking for the ministers. There is scarce a day passes over but somebody will ask me,—'When will the minister come?'"

How many of Dr. Wheelock's Indian students actually became schoolmasters we can not tell, but at one time eight are spoken of as thus engaged, with 127 children under their care. Some of these youth gave evidence of true piety, and entered upon this work in the spirit of missionaries. As an illustration of this, take these words of Joseph Wooley, a schoolmaster among the Mohawks: "The language of my heart is, to contribute the little mite I have to the living God, and be in his service. My soul seems to be more and more upon the perishing pagans in these woods. I long for the conversion of their souls, and that they may come to the knowledge of our Lord Jesus Christ, and be saved. I wish I was made able to teach and instruct them, and I shall do whatever lies in my power to tell them of Christ as long as I tarry."

Among those who sought instruction at this school was the celebrated Mohawk chief, Joseph Brant. He was born in 1742, and, with other Indian youth, was sent here by Sir William Johnson. Espousing, as was most natural, the cause of the English against the Revolutionists, he became the formidable enemy of the American forces. Wise in council, brave in action, and a terror to his adversaries, yet he was not without magnanimity as a warrior. In the work of missions among his people, he rendered very essential service, becoming an interpreter to the missionaries, and assisting them in other ways, making his house an asylum for them in the wilderness. About the year 1772 he united with the church and was very zealous in his efforts to christianize his people. At the close of the Revolutionary struggle he directed his attention particularly to the social and moral elevation of the Indians, in which work he had great obstacles to oppose. He endeavored to secure for them systematic religious instruction. He was disposed, at one time, to acquire a knowledge of the Greek language, in order to make a more accurate translation of the New Testament into his native tongue. While in England he published the "Book of Common Prayer," and the gospel of Mark, in Mohawk and English, and he there collected funds for the first Episcopal church which was built in Canada West. He died with a triumphant Christian faith, November 24, 1807, at the age of sixty-five.

Of the English students in Dr. Wheelock's school, the first who went out as a missionary to the Indians, was Rev. Charles Jeffrey Smith. He was graduated at Yale College, in 1757, and was ordained as a missionary in Lebanon Crank, in 1763. After a short period of service among the Indians, he went to Virginia, to labor for the instruction of the slaves. He was subject to a disease which caused violent pain in the head, and while on a visit to Long Island he went out with his gun on the morning of August 10, 1770, and was soon found dead, under circumstances indicating that he had shot himself.

Samuel Kirkland, son of Rev. Daniel Kirkland, pastor of the third Congregational Church in Norwich, (now Lisbon,) was born at Norwich, December 1, 1741. At the age of twenty, he entered this school; was graduated at Princeton College, New Jersey, in 1765, leaving College a few months before graduation to engage in his mission to the Indians; a work to which he had given himself from very early life. In company with two Seneca Indians, he set out, November 20, 1764, on a missionary expedition to their own tribe, the most remote and the most savage of the Six Nations. The snow was four feet deep, and he traveled on snow-shoes, with his pack of provisions on his back, more than two hundred miles into the wilderness, without paths or houses to lodge in.

After an absence of about a year and a half, a period of great hardship and peril, yet of some encouragement in his work, he returned to Connecticut, bringing a Seneca chief with him.

On the 19th of June, 1766, he was ordained at Lebanon Crank, and on the same day received a general commission as an Indian Missionary from the Connecticut "Board of Correspondents" of the Society in Scotland for Propagating Christian Knowledge; a board which was constituted July 4, 1764, to have the supervision of these Indian missions. In about six weeks he was again at his mission work, taking up his residence among the Oneidas, where he continued to labor, with some interruptions, for more than forty years. A Christian church was soon organized under his ministrations, which, by occasional accessions, showed a good degree of prosperity. His labors were partially suspended during the Revolutionary war, though he continued to hold such an influence as to keep the Oneidas and part of the Mohawks on friendly terms with the Americans, while nearly all in the other tribes of the Six Nations took the position of active hostility. In 1779 he was Brigade Chaplain with General Sullivan, having previously been employed in procuring intelligence of the designs and movements of the enemy at Niagara. In the spring of 1784 he resumed his missionary work at Oneida. Two years afterwards his labors were attended with a considerable revival of religion, which seemed to have its beginning in the conversion of a strong minded Indian more than seventy years old, who up to that time had been a bigoted pagan.

In 1788, Mr. Kirkland and his two eldest sons received from the Indians and the State of New York conjointly, a grant of large and valuable tracts of land in the vicinity of Oneida, on which he built for himself a log house. In 1790, while on a mission to Congress in behalf of the Senecas, he was instrumental in the conversion of the celebrated chief, Cornplanter, to the Christian faith. "In the winter of 1791–2, by request of the Secretary of War, he conducted about forty chiefs and warriors, a representation of five nations, to Philadelphia, to consult with Congress on the best method of introducing the blessings of civilization among them, and also with a view of preserving peace between the Indians and the United States. This visit had the desired effect, and not only secured to the United States the friendship of the Six Nations, rendering them mediators between the Federal Government and the Western Indians, but also securing to the Six Nations an increased degree of favor from the Government in the promotion of education and civilization among them."

In 1793 Mr. Kirkland accomplished what had long been a favorite object with him, in securing a charter for an institution under the name of Hamilton Oneida Academy, to which he made a donation of several hundred acres of land. This Academy, in 1812, four years after his death, was exalted to the rank of a College, in the first class of which, at graduation, with only one associate, was the Rev. George A. Calhoun, D. D., of North Coventry. This is now Hamilton College, at Clinton, New York.

Mr. Kirkland continued his labors among the Indians as he was able, and died February 28, 1808, aged sixty-six. His son, John Thornton Kirkland, was President of Harvard University from 1810 to 1828. He is the only missionary from Dr. Wheelock's school who spent his whole life among the Indians. Several others were distinctly set apart to this work, but during the distractions of the war, and from other influences, their connection with the work was of short duration.

Among these were Messrs. Titus Smith and Theophilus Chamberlain, who were ordained as missionaries April 24, 1765, the latter graduating at Yale College in the same year, and the former in the year next preceding. They were with Dr. Wheelock several months, to prepare for the mission. Mr. Chamberlain had formerly been taken captive by the Indians, and became so much interested in their welfare that he spent all his property and ran in debt in order to fit himself to preach the gospel among them.

Mr. Sylvanus Ripley was early ordained as a missionary to the Indians. After his labors were closed in that capacity, he took the charge of the mission school, then connected with

Dartmouth College. In 1782 he became Professor of Divinity in the College, and succeeded Dr. Wheelock in the pastoral charge of the students and the inhabitants of the village of Hanover.

Levi Frisbie, born in Branford, April, 1748, was placed under the care of Dr. Wheelock in 1767, with a view to his becoming a missionary. He was graduated at Dartmouth College in 1771. In the two following years he was engaged in a mission to the Delaware Indians. He was ordained in 1775, and continued in his mission work till broken off by the distracted state of the country. He was settled over the first church in Ipswich, Massachusetts, February 7, 1776, where he remained thirty years, and died February 25, 1806, at the age of fifty-eight.

In company with Mr. Frisbie, David McClure was also engaged in the mission among the Delawares. He was born at Newport, Rhode Island, November 18, 1748. His youthful days were spent chiefly in Boston, in the school of the famous "Master Lovell." At the age of fifteen he became a member of Dr. Wheelock's school with a view to engage as a missionary among the Indians. He was graduated at Yale College in 1769. He was ordained May 20, 1772, and after the experience of a few months in the missionary work was compelled to desist because of the war. After a ministry of nine years in Northampton, Massachusetts, he was installed pastor of the church in East Windsor, (now South Windsor,) June 11, 1786, where he died June 25, 1820, aged seventy-one, having held the pastoral office there thirty-four years.

David Avery, born in Franklin, April 5, 1746, was also, for a short time, engaged in this missionary work. He was hopefully converted under the preaching of Whitfield; was fitted for College in Dr. Wheelock's school; was graduated at Yale College in 1769; and was ordained as missionary to the Oneida Indians as colleague with Rev. Mr. Kirkland. In consequence of an injury received, he was soon obliged to leave the mission; and after preaching on Long Island a short time, he was settled over a church in Gaysboro, (now Windsor,) Vermont, March 25, 1773. The Sabbath after the news of the battle of

Lexington reached his place, he preached his farewell sermon, telling the people that God would take care of them; as for himself he was going to join the army. When the congregation was dismissed, he took his stand upon the steps and gave a soul-stirring address in behalf of his country, entreating his people, "by every motive of patriotism, and as they valued liberty and abhorred slavery, not to turn a deaf ear to her cry." Twenty of his parishioners gave a quick response to his appeal, chose him captain, shouldered their muskets and started on foot for Boston, and in ten days from the battle at Lexington they were in their camp at Cambridge. The next day, which was the Sabbath, standing upon a temporary stage, formed by turning up a rum hogshead, in the area of Cambridge College, he preached from Nehemiah 4; 14, "And I looked, and rose up, and said unto the nobles and rulers, and to the rest of the people, Be not afraid of them; remember the Lord which is great and terrible, and fight for your brethren, your sons and your daughters, your wives and your homes." While holding his position as captain, he instituted daily religious services, going from tent to tent to read the word of God.

He was at the battle of Bunker Hill; saw the defeat of our army at the battle of Long Island; was by the side of Washington in his melancholy retreat through the Jerseys; was present at the taking of Burgoyne, at the capture of the Hessians at Trenton, and in the battle of Princeton; was in the army during that terrible winter at Valley Forge; helped build the fortifications at Ticonderoga; was by the side of Washington when he signed the death warrant of Andre, and witnessed the execution of that ill-fated British officer; and was very active in the efforts which were made to capture the traitor Arnold. Having served his country as captain and afterwards as chaplain from the beginning to the end of the war, he preached successively at Bennington, Vermont, at Wrentham, Massachusetts, and Chaplin, Connecticut, and died in September, 1818, aged seventy-two.

This missionary enterprize among the Indians was begun with much promise; was carried on in the face of increasing obstacles, with a true Christian and commendable zeal, and if it did not reach the full anticipations, this must be attributed in part to the on-coming Revolutionary struggle, and in part to the impracticability of turning the Indian character to very extensive service in the work of missions. How much good was actually accomplished,—how many of those Indian souls were turned from paganism to the saving reception of Christ, eternity alone can reveal. It is to be noticed that the success which attended these early missionary efforts among the Indians is very much like the success which has attended the efforts of later days. They are an unsettled roving people, and if any thing is to be done for their spiritual welfare, it must be done under these unfavorable circumstances. And no one can say that *all* that has been done for them is not fully justified by the actual spiritual renovation which, in individual instances, may have been wrought by the Spirit and the Word.

TRIBUTE TO THE MEMORY OF REV. E. WHEELOCK, D. D., FOUNDER OF MOOR'S CHARITY SCHOOL AND DARTMOUTH COLLEGE.

By Dr. O. B. Lyman.

The past in scanning, much we often find,
To please and interest the inquiring mind:
Old things not always are devoid of worth,
When found connected with one's place of birth;
And often, light upon the mind is cast,
As we compare the Present with the Past.

We plant an acorn—'tis a little thing—
A little plant will from that acorn spring;
In a few years will rise above our heads
A giant oak, that wide its branches spreads,
Destined to stand perhaps a thousand years,
'Mid storm and calm—at last it disappears.

One hundred years ago, a man of worth,
With a big heart—Old Windham gave him birth—
Started in Lebanon—Columbia now the name—
A little school the forest sons to tame:
Here the poor Indian sought for mental food,
Here Occum found, that God was righteous, good:
That pale men too, instruction here received,
Here sought the truth, here found, and here believed.
Here Occum was prepared to preach the Word,
And set before his race his dying Lord:
Hence too he went to visit England's shore,
Preach to her king—sight never seen before.
From this, the thought in WHEELOCK's mind arose,
To found a College ere his life should close,
Where the poor pagan might be led to find
Light, food and drink, for his benighted mind,
As well as he who wears a lighter skin,
But has a soul as deeply stained with sin.
Thus *Dartmouth's* seed was sown and sprouted here,
At least, in *Wheelock's* mind, with fervent prayer.

He now before his people laid his plan,
Elsewhere, to consummate the work began.
With deep regret they heard his earnest plea,
Reluctantly consent it might so be.*
From the great work he could not well be turned,
His heart for it with love increasing burned.
Occum had touched a chord in England's heart,
Thrilling it with sympathy in every part.
Its warmest friend Lord Dartmouth soon became,
And hence the institution took its name.
King George himself enchanted with the theme,
Became a donor to the glorious scheme,
And by his lords and men of high renown,
The same good feeling for the cause was shown:
Wheelock was moved with an increase of toil,
To transplant Dartmouth to a northern soil,
And like Elisha in the wilderness,
A school of Prophets found that God would bless:
So hence to Hampshire 'neath her lofty pine,
That gleam and sing in light and notes divine,
Removed from hills, on an extensive plain,
Where undisturbed the school might long remain,
There like a Patriarch, he, full of years,
Planted and watered Dartmouth with his tears:
Yes, lived to see her rooted deep and strong,
With every prospect of her living long.
Like Solomon's father, what he had begun,
To finish up, he left behind, his son:
Like good old Simeon, serene and calm,
His infant school now resting on his arm,—
His arm of faith, upheld by God's free grace.
He now could say, "let me depart in peace!"
His course thus finished, like a star at even,
He sank to rest, a brilliant gem of heaven!

Thus, as the oak that from the acorn sprung,
Has towered high, its branches wide outflung,
So Dartmouth stands, though small indeed at birth,
A school matured and full of sterling worth:
A monument bespeaking noblest praise,
To Wheelock's memory, in remotest days.

---

* See Note A, Appendix.

STATEMENTS AND STATISTICS.

By Rev. William H. Moore.

The population of your town in 1840 was 842; in 1860, 854,—a gain of twelve.

It is worthy of notice that your church has so generally been supplied with pastors, not having been destitute over fifteen years in 150.

Twelve revivals are named since 1780, or, on an average, one in seven years.

Sixteen ministers have been raised up from this parish,—one in ten years, and it has thus furnished about 300 years of ministerial service in Connecticut, and about 175 years outside of Connecticut, including forty-four years among the heathen;—making about 475 years in all.

In January 1, 1832, the church reported 155 members, which included the addition by the revival of 1831; which, namely, forty-one, being deducted would leave the membership before the revival, 114. In January 1, 1866, there were 132 members, or fifteen per cent. of the population. The fruits of the present revival will increase the ratio to twenty per cent.

The General Association has published the statistics of the churches for thirty-five years, beginning in 1832. In seven of these years your church made no report; in twenty-eight years they made reports. In eleven of these none were added by profession; in twenty-six of them infants were baptized. In the twenty-eight years reported, 165 came in by profession, or six a year; and seventy-six died, or three a year; the professions being double the deaths, which is a good record. In -these years there came in by letter, fifty-one; went out by letter, fifty; which shows that the church does not diminish from this source. Dividing these years into two periods of fourteen each, we find that the deaths in the two periods are nearly equal, thirty-seven and thirty-nine; as well as the infant baptisms, fifty-seven and fifty-eight. The ratio of infants baptized to a thousand members, is thirty-one. You ought to be gratified with this record on infant baptism. And I hope the ratio will not fall during the administration of your present pastor, and that that may exceed the term of any of his predecessors.

APPENDIX.

PROCEEDINGS AND ORDER OF EXERCISES.

Some time in the year 1865 the question was asked, Shall the celebration of the one hundred and fiftieth anniversary of the formation of the Church in Columbia be observed? A general public sentiment seemed to answer—Yes. This event was to occur some time in the year 1866, the precise date of which could not be ascertained, but still no special action was taken towards the furtherance of this desire until June 29th, 1866, when it was "voted by the church to have an anniversary celebration the present year, it being the one hundred and fiftieth year since the organization of the church and ecclesiastical society in this place," and at the same time

"Rev. Frederick D. Avery,

John S. Yeomans,

William B. Little,

Deac. Chester W. Lyman, and

David D. Little,

were appointed a committee to make preliminary arrangements.

Requests were also made to Rev. F. D. Avery and John S. Yeomans to prepare Historical Papers relating to the early history of the Church and Society.

The committee of arrangements subsequently met and fixed upon the 24th day of October as the day of celebration. They also decided to have a general collation, and for the furtherance of this object appointed

William H. Yeomans,

Silas H. Dewey,

Henry E. Lyman,

Daniel T. Fuller,

Samuel B. West, and

James P. Little,

a committee on collation.

They also appointed Samuel F. West, Esq., to be President of the day, and arranged their order of exercises.

ORDER OF EXERCISES.

MORNING.

Voluntary; Anthem,—Praise God from whom all blessings flow.

Reading of Scriptures by the Pastor.

HYMN.

Tune, Boylston.

1. Great is the Lord our God,
    And let his praise be great;
    He makes his churches his abode,
    His most delightful seat.

2. These temples of his grace,
    How beautiful they stand!
    The honors of our native place,
    And bulwarks of our land.

3. In Zion God is known,
    A refuge in distress:
    How bright hath his salvation shone,
    Through all her palaces!

4. Oft have our fathers told,
    Our eyes have often seen,
    How well our God secures the fold,
    Where his own sheep have been.

5. In every new distress,
    We'll to his house repair,
    We'll think upon his wondrous grace,
    And seek deliverance there.

Prayer by Rev. S. G. WILLARD, of Willimantic.

ANNIVERSARY HYMN.

Words by Doct. O. B. LYMAN, of Hartford.

Tune, Salome.

1. Since this fair branch from yonder vine,
    Was plucked and planted in this soil,
    And since was built this holy shrine,
    'Midst earnest prayer and praise and toil,
    One hundred fifty years have fled;
    The fathers sleep now with the dead.

2. Great God! we tread these courts to-day,
    To celebrate that hour divine,
When our forefathers led the way,
    To plant and rear this precious vine;
This vine they watered with their tears,
That fruit might grow in future years.

3. It has been watched and pruned and kept,
    Through God's dear children until now,
Here they have praised and prayed and wept,
    And here submissive still they bow;
Still earnestly they press their suit,
That it may bear much precious fruit.

4. Here sinners too are wont to cry
    For mercy to our father's God,
That he would hear them from on high,
    And stay yet his avenging rod;
Oh God of Love! incline thine ear,
The suppliant's earnest prayer to hear.

5. And as the years roll swiftly on,
    To make complete this century too,
And we our labors shall have done,
    And bid the scenes of earth adieu,
Still may this branch, this precious vine,
Bear for our children fruit divine.

Reading of the original petition of the people to be set off a society, by JAMES P. LITTLE.

Historical Sketch,—The Pastors of the Church, by Rev. F. D. AVERY.

HYMN.

Tune, Exhortation.

1. Let saints below in concert sing,
    With those to glory gone:
For all the servants of our King,
    In earth and heaven are one.

2. One family we dwell in him,
    One church above, beneath,
Though now divided by the stream,
    The narrow stream of death:

10

3. One army of the living God,
   To his command we bow;
   Part of the host have crossed the flood,
   And part are crossing now.

4. Some to their everlasting home,
   This solemn moment fly;
   And we are to the margin come,
   And soon expect to die.

5. Lord Jesus be our constant guide;
   And, when the word is given,
   Bid death's cold flood its waves divide,
   And land us safe in heaven.

Historical Paper,—Meeting Houses, by J. S. YEOMANS.
Recess to partake of collation.

AFTERNOON.

Historical Papers,—Education, Music, and Miscellaneous, by J. S. YEOMANS.

HYMN.
Tune, Bridgewater.

1. The Saviour, when to heaven he rose,
   In splendid triumph o'er his foes,
   Scattered his gifts on men below,
   And wide his royal bounties flow.

2. Hence sprung the apostles' honored name,
   Sacred beyond heroic fame:
   In lowlier forms to bless our eyes,
   Pastors from hence, and teachers rise.

3. So shall the bright succession run,
   Through the last courses of the sun;
   While unborn churches, by their care,
   Shall rise and flourish, large and fair.

4. Jesus, our Lord, their hearts shall know,
   The spring whence all these blessings flow;
   Pastors and people shout his praise,
   Through the long round of endless days.

Ministers raised in the Parish, by Rev. F. D. AVERY.

Address,—Reminiscences of Columbia, by Rev. C. LITTLE, of Woodbury.

Address, by Rev. W. H. MOORE, of Berlin.

HYMN.

Tune, Coronation.

1. All hail the power of Jesus' name!
   Let angels prostrate fall;
   Bring forth the royal diadem,
   And crown him Lord of all.

2. Crown him, ye martyrs of our God,
   Who from his altar call;
   Hail him who saves you by his blood,
   And crown him Lord of all.

3. Sinners, whose love can ne'er forget,
   The wormwood and the gall,—
   Go, spread your trophies at his feet,
   And crown him Lord of all.

4. Let every kindred, every tribe,
   On this terrestrial ball,
   To him all majesty ascribe,
   And crown him Lord of all.

Historical Papers,—The Deacons,—Moor's Indian Charity School, by Rev. F. D. AVERY.

Voluntary; Anthem,—Before Jehovah's awful throne.

Poems, by Doctor O. B. LYMAN, of Hartford.

Remarks by Rev. Mr. PIKE, of Marlborough.

Remarks, by Rev. S. G. WILLARD, of Willimantic, and Rev. F. WILLIAMS, of Chaplin.

Prayer, by Rev. F. WILLIAMS, of Chaplin.

DOXOLOGY.

Praise God from whom all blessings flow!
Praise Him, all creatures here below!
Praise Him above, ye heavenly host:
Praise Father, Son, and Holy Ghost.

BENEDICTION.

At a meeting of the Church, held October 26th, 1866, it was voted that the Exercises of the Celebration be published, and

JOHN S. YEOMANS,

SAMUEL F. WEST, and

Rev. F. D. AVERY,

were appointed a committee to superintend the publication.

At a meeting of the Ecclesiastical Society, held October 27th, 1866, it was voted that the Society committee, consisting of

ASHER K. FULLER,

HORATIO W. LITTLE, and

JOHN A. HUTCHINS,

act with the committee appointed by the Church upon the matter of the publication.

THE COLLATION.

Owing to the lateness of the season it became necessary that the Collation should be dispensed at the Town Hall. And through the untiring energy of the committee whose business it was to arrange this portion of the exercises, it was made *one* of the *attractions* of the day. This committee at one of their meetings appointed a sub-committee to assist in the distribution of the refreshments, consisting of the following named persons: ·

CHARLES H. CLARK,	Miss SOPHIA C. YEOMANS,
JAMES L. DOWNER,	Miss EMILY J. LITTLE,
Mrs. SILAS H. DEWEY,	Miss ESTHER HUTCHINS,
Mrs. CHARLES H. CLARK,	Miss EMILY A. WRIGHT,
Mrs. WILLIAM H. YEOMANS,	Miss AMELIA J. FULLER,
Mrs. HENRY G. WOODWORTH,	Miss MARY D. LITTLE,
Mrs. DANIEL T. FULLER,	Miss MARY DANIELS.

According to request, at an early hour of the day of the celebration, the good things, requisite to sate the appetite, began to flow in from all parts of the town, which continued until all the space apportioned to that purpose was literally filled to overflowing; so that the committee were enabled to make a "Bill of Fare," consisting of the following:

Cold Tongue, Baked Lamb, (stuffed,) Sandwiches, Wheat Bread, Fruit Cake, Silver Cake, Cookies, Apple Pie, Cream Pie, Apples, Sliced Beef Ham, Cold Chicken, Biscuit, Loaf Cake, Gold Cake, Cup Cakes, Fried Cakes, Mince Pie, Corn Starch Pie, Baked Apples, Coffee.

Much of the cake was beautifully trimmed, showing the artistic taste of the ladies of 1866. The tables were also decorated with bouquets of flowers. As the hour of repast arrived, the citizens and strangers repaired to the hall, preceded by the President and Clergymen present, where after order was restored, a blessing was invoked by Rev. William J. Jennings, of North Coventry, and the wants of the inner man were bountifully supplied.

The fragments remaining, were distributed among the needy; thereby filling *their* hearts with thankfulness, that it was put into the minds of the people, to celebrate the one hundred and fiftieth anniversary of the formation of the Church and Society of Columbia.

COPY OF ORIGINAL PETITION OF THE PEOPLE TO BE SET OFF A SOCIETY.

To ye inhabitants of Lebanon the humble petition of us whose Names are under written inhabiting at a place called the crank and at Hop river and ajacent to ye crank with some others that have a right of land near sd Crank. Humbly showeth that whereas the providence of God who bounds our habitations hath so ordered our settlement in the world so remote from ye publick worship of God, which we and ours stand in great need of w^c by Reason of ye Remoteness of the place of worship, which way ever we goe, that there are but few of our families can constantly attend and we being got to such a number of families that are here and preparing to come among us that we hope that in case you that are our fathers, breathren & Christian friends in Lebanon would be pleased to grant us with ye accommodation of part of y^o land in the Township of Lebanon w^c we might have ye worship of God set up among us in some short time w^c we hope, we greatly desire & shall indeaver after, according as ye providence of God shall lead in that matter; and we hope and are confident that you would do for us w^t you can that may be reasonable for to incorage & promote so good a work. We therefore desire and intreat you who are our fathers, brethren and Christian friends in s^d Lebanon to consider our case & do what you can conveniently to promote such a good work & set out to us for ye promoting of a sociaty heare, as much of your Township as may be incoueging for ye same. We dont here pretend to be our owne carvers but desire and request of you that a line may be run from y⁰ North Pond the westerly line of y⁰ five mile to y⁰ great Cheast-nutt tree on Cheastnutt Hil, which is the Northerly corner of y⁰ five mile; then to turn eastward in the line of y⁰ five mile to y⁰ southarly branch of ten mile brook so down by y⁰ brook as the brook runs to (the) y⁰ eastward part of y⁰ town bounds to be, to incorieg the above sd sociaty, but in case you canot comply with y⁰ above sd line takcing in all the Land in y⁰ town bounds towards hebron & windham we then desire your compliance, in any other line that you may se cause to afford us for y⁰ incorieging so good a work; we also desire and crave your holys with respect of gaining in to y⁰ Township that land lying between Lebanon bounds & Coventry or so much of it as you may judge nesesary for to obtain y⁰ end above sd; and it seems needful that there be speedy care taken about those of us that live out of y⁰ bounds of Lebanon that they be brought into the bounds, for we understand in case nothing be propounded to further & promote y⁰ motion above sd, that our friends at Coventry do intend to petition the Generall Court that such of us as are out of y⁰ bounds of Lebanon might be annexed to Coventry, & if it be once don their may be aboundance of more difficulty in bringing about the designe above sd, and further, seince it is so that we or y⁰ most of us must attend it & we be thereby forc⁴ to do it we pray that we may be freed from paying to y⁰ ministery in Lebanon; and also that provided we are incorieged in so good a work as y⁰ settling of a sosiaty heare that we in a short time be at Charge towards y⁰ settling of a minister heare by building, breaking up of Land & forming of it in that we thereby may incorieg a minister to settle among us; we then desire our publick taxes as to town charges might be also Released to us all, w⁰ we hope you will Readaly Grant to us your Humble petitioners; and in so doing you will greatly oblige us who are your friends & Neighbours.

Leb, february ye 28th, 1714-15.

Richard Mason, Josiah Loomis, Jr., Benjamin Woodworth, Charles Dowolf, Josiah Loomis, Henry Woodworth, Benony Clark, Ebenezer Richardson, Ezekiell Woodworth, Isaac Tilden, Joseph Clark, Ephraim Sprague, Benjⁿ Woodworth, Jr., Samˡˡ Wright, John Sweetland, Josiah Lyman, Thomas Porter, Ebenezer Woodworth, Joseph Fowler, Ephraim Tupper, Caleb Loomis, Benjaⁿ Small, Nathˡˡ Dewey, Thomas Woodward.

April the 26th, 1715, at a Legall town Meting of yᵉ inhabitance of Lebanon they then granted the petition of yᵉ people at yᵉ Crank either to be a sosiaty by themselves or a township according as the honoured Courte shall see cause to incorieg either for a sosiaty or a township, allways provided that yᵉ town Reserve to yᵐ selves all yᵉ Right of Land in sd tract, both alottments & Comon Right as to yᵉ, for yᵉ land & also exept petitionning for an adition between Coventry & Lebanon, and also provided there be no publick taxes Layd on yᵉ Land untill yᵉ Land be improved as yᵉ Law directs & also whereas the petitioners to hᵉ all the land on the westerly side of yᵉ five mile it is agreed & we do alow they shall goe southwards on yᵉ west side of yᵉ five mile, so far as Hebron Road from Lebanon; likewise provided they pay publick taxes to yᵉ town untill they have liberty & incoriegement from the Generall Courte to be a sosiaty or township by themselves, the above written was voted by the town; at the same time Stephen Tilden, Joseph Owen, John Huchison, Joseph Hutchinson, Joseph Owen, Jun., & Moses Owen, all entered their protest against the above sd vote.

COPY OF A RATE BILL FOR THE NORTH PARISH OF LEBA-NON, (NOW COLUMBIA,) FOR THE YEAR 1741, TO PAY THE SALARY OF REV. ELEAZER WHEELOCK.

The Sume total of this Reat Bill | is £330–16–09 made for the Defra | ing the Nescrary Charges In yᵉ North | Parish in Lebanon Atested by us in | yᵉ year 1741 |

ELIAKIM TUPPER, } Comite.
JOHN NEWCOMB, }

To Joseph Paine, Collector of | Raits for yᵉ North Parish in | Lebanon this are to order you | to Collect and Geather this Raite | of Each man his Portion as is set | Down in this Reate Bill and | you are to Geather it by yᵉ | first day of January Next | and you are to Pay it unto yᵉ | Reved Mʳ Eleazer Wheelock yᵉ | Sume of 290 by yᵉ first Day of | January next and yᵉ Rest of yᵉ | money you are to Pay unto Mʳ John | Sims by yᵉ Same time and this | Shall be your order December | yᵉ 14 AD. 1741.

ELIAKIM TUPPER, } Comite.
JOHN NEWCOMB, }

The Sum total of this Rate bill Except yᵉ | Dooms if I Cast Right is £324–19–0 | Test.   E. WHEELOCK.

	£	s.	d.		£	s.	d.
Samuel Allen	4	02	11	Benj: Fuler	3	01	01
Robert Avery	1	19	10	Amos Fuller	2	05	09
Joshua Allan, Jur.	2	01	08	Benj: Fuller, Ju':	1	01	11
Joshua Allen	1	07	02	Amos Fuller, Jun'	0	16	08
John Allen	1	19	06	Jeremiah Futer	0	18	05
Samu¹ Allen, Jun.	0	17	06	Noah Fuller	0	18	05
Samu¹ Buckengham	4	14	06	Henry Glover	3	01	11
Jeams Brigs	3	02	01	William Gager	2	15	06
Jeams Bill	3	15	08	Samuel Guilds	1	15	10
Samuel Breuster	3	01	03	John Gibbs	3	05	05
Benj: Ball	1	17	05	Henry Glover, Jun'	1	15	00
Saxton Baly	2	05	10	Samuel Guilds, Juner	0	19	09
Jedediah Bill	0	17	06	Ebenezer Gray, Esquire	0	07	05
Philip Bill	3	01	00	Samuel Hatchenson	1	01	08
Elisha Bill	0	18	05	Nathanel House	2	08	00
Ebenezer Ball	0	15	09	Israel Guilds	2	07	00
Joseph Clark	7	10	01	Walter Harris	2	09	00
Benony Clark	4	15	00	Nathaniel Hide	0	06	00
Nehemiah Clason	2	18	08	Eleazer Hutchenson	4	07	08
Beenj: Collins	4	18	00	Stephen Hutchenson	2	09	01
Solomon Curtis	3	02	10	Jo" hutchenson	2	00	00
Dudatus Curtis	0	15	09	Tim: Hutchenson	2	02	04
Nathaniel Curtis	0	13	08	Abel Hole Brook	1	13	05
Joen Claseon	1	05	15	Nathaniel House, Ju'	2	00	01
Nathan Claseon	0	18	05	Stephen hunt	2	02	09
Danel Church	0	00	06	Willim: Hunt	2	17	07
Eleazer Curtis	0	18	05	John house	1	14	02
John Dogit	3	09	02	Samul House	1	01	06
John Damond	2	05	11	Gideon House	0	15	09
Henry Dyre	1	17	01	Nathanel knap	0	07	00
Joseph Davis	1	14	01	Richard Lyman	2	16	01
Nathaniel Dewey	0	05	01	Josiah Lyman	3	08	02
Sam¹ Dunham	1	01	13	Joseph Loomis,	1	14	00
Sam¹ Dewey	0	02	11	Benony Loomis	1	05	05
John Damond, Jun'	1	01	11	Nathanel Lomis	1	09	07
Jonathan Dewey	1	02	09	Caleb Loomis	1	14	05
Joseph Dewey	1	14	09	Tomas Lyman	2	03	01˙
Moses Dewey	0	15	09	David Lyman	1	07	09
Richard English	2	01	02	John Loomis	0	12	03
John English	1	01	00	Danel Lee	1	10	08
				Ephraim Loomis	1	01	00

Ichabod Maxfield	1	07	02	Joseph Swet Land	2 12 02
Isaac Merit	1	13	01	Elijah Sprauge	1 15 11
Peter mesusan	0	16	08	Jeams Smalley	2 01 02
Linsford mory	2	11	07	Eliakim Tupper	3 16 08
John Newcomb	5	11	02	Stephen Tuttle	1 08 02
Samuel Negus	2	06	05	Jeams tuttle	0 19 08
Eddy Newcomb	1	06	03	Elias Tupper	1 03 08
Josiah Owen	0	19	03	Ebenezer Tomas	0 05 03
Thomas Porter	4	18	00	Ezekel Tomas	2 19 05
Joseph Paine	3	16	02	william Vallence	1 17 05
John Porter	3	11	06	Henry woodward	4 05 09
Josiah Phiny	2	17	11	Nathanel white	4 13 05
Jeams Pinno	3	04	01	Thomas wooward	3 02 09
Samuel Porter	2	05	07	Ebenezer woodwarth	4 19 04
Jeames Pease	2	08	03	Benj: woodwarth	2 14 06
Joseph Pinno	0	18	05	Ichabod woodworth	3 16 00
Samuel Parker	2	13	02	Amos woodwarth	2 03 04
Joshua Phinney	1	09	04	Ezekel woodwarth	2 03 10
william Phinney	1	00	03	Samuel woodward	2 07 03
John Pitkin	0	05	07	Israel woodward	3 19 09
Israel Post	0	12	03	Jeams wright	2 07 00
Phineas Post	3	03	00	Thomas white	1 04 02
Amos Randal	1	14	10	Noah webster	1 15 05
David Royce	1	08	11	Preserved wright	2 04 03
mathew Royce	1	18	09	Ebenezer woodwarth, Jr.	1 01 00
Ephraim Sprague	4	04	11	Nathanel wright	1 11 00
John Sims	4	08	05	Ebenezer wright	1 00 00
John Sollard	3	01	00	Samuel wright	2 04 06
John Swet Land	3	17	11	Benony wright	1 02 09
Benj: Smaley	5	00	02	Henry woodward, Juner.	0 13 09
John Sims, Junr.	2	08	08	Ebenezer Richardson	4 16 01
william Sims	2	07	07	Youngs	0 03 07
Peleg Spraug	0	18	05	Noah Dewey	1 19 01
Perez Spraug	2	00	08	Philip Bill his Doome	
william Swift	2	09	00	Rate for Estate not	
Joseph Smaley	2	00	03	Given in	0 03 00
George Sims	1	09	09	Captin Buckengham is	
John Sprauge	0	02	10	Doomed for Estate	
Benj: Swet Land	1	02	09	not Given in	0 11 11
John Sweet Land, Junr	1	08	02		

11

MEMBERS OF THE CHURCH,

January, 1867.

Rev. Frederick D. Avery. }
Mrs. Charlotte M. Avery. }
  " Lucina C. Armstrong,
  " Lucretia B. Avery,
  " Sally E. Abell.

Mrs. Sophia Barstow.
Henry W. Buell, }
Mrs. Nancy Buell. }
  " Harriet E. Button,
Charlotte J. Brown,
Alice L. Brown.
Fannie W. Bascom.

William Collins, }
Mrs. Roxana Collins, }
Joseph Clark. }
Mrs. Margaret Clark, }
  " Mary Clark.
Lyman C. Clark, }
Mrs. Cynthia Clark. }
Willard B. Clark, }
Mrs. Lucy F. Clark, }
Charles H. Clark, }
Mrs. Caroline O. Clark, }
  " Clarissa Clark,
Samuel A. Collins,
William A. Collins,
Jane A. Collins,
Louisa Chenery.

Eleazer Dewey,
Dea. Lorenzo W. Dewey, }
Mrs. Lucy Dewey, }
Elmore G. Dewey, }
Mrs. Elizabeth C. Dewey, }
Silas H. Dewey.
Mrs. Nancy M. Dewey,
  " Sarah A. Dewey,
Catharine A. Dewey.

Jonathan C. Fuller, }
Mrs. Nancy A. Fuller, }
Charles R. Fuller, }
Mrs. Sophia Fuller, }

Amasa B. Fuller. }
Mrs. Minerva A. Fuller, }
Alanson H. Fuller, }
Mrs. Mary L. Fuller, }
Asher K. Fuller, }
Mrs. Caroline A. Fuller. }
George B. Fuller, }
Mrs. Jane E. Fuller. }
Daniel T. Fuller, }
Mrs. M. Amelia Fuller, }
  " Naomi Fuller,
Gilbert Fuller,
Wealthy Fuller,
Orrilla Fuller,
Amelia J. Fuller,
Ozro D. Fuller.

Mrs. Mindwell Holbrook,
  " Elizabeth M. Hunt,
  " Nancy Holbrook,
  " Betsey A. Hunt,
  " Sarah B. Hunt,
  " Eliza F. Hutchins,
  " Jane Holbrook,
  " Eliza Hartson,
  " Elizabeth J. Holbrook,
Anson Holbrook,
Olivia Holbrook,
John A. Hutchins, }
Mrs. Gertrude M. Hutchins, }
Joseph Hutchins,
Mrs. Lucy W. Holt.
Esther Hutchins,
Eliza A. Hutchins,
Alice M. Holbrook,
L. Huldah Holbrook,
Ellen E. Holbrook,
Lucy J. Holbrook.

Shubael S. Isham, }
Mrs. Mary A. Isham. }

Dea. Benjamin Lyman,
  " Chester W. Lyman, }
Mrs. Cornelia E. Lyman, }

Mrs. Sophia Lyman.
Mrs. Nancy Little,
Norman Little,
Benjamin W. Lyman,
Mrs. Wealthy Little,
Lydia Lyman,
Lucina W. Lyman,
Samuel Little,
William B. Little, }
Mrs. Harriet P. Little. {
Horatio W. Little, }
Mrs. Esther E. Little. {
David D. Little, }
Mrs. Maria J. Little. {
Norman P. Little. }
Mrs. Mary Ann Little. {
Giles Little, }
Mrs. Cynthia A. Little, {
James P. Little,
Emily J. Little,
Hubert Little,
Myron W. Little,
Samuel E. Lyman, }
Mrs. Fannie C. Lyman, }
Alfred W. Lyman. }
Mrs. Elizabeth C. Lyman, }
Charlotte H. Little,
Mary D. Little,
Henry E. Lyman,
Chester B. Lyman.

Mrs. Sally Manley,
"   Martha G. McIntosh,
George W. Morgan,
Adelaide M. Morgan.

Mrs. Harriet Nye.

Mary J. Osborne.

Mrs. Saxsy Perry,
"   Clarissa F. Porter,
Augustus Post. }
Mrs. Betsey G. Post, {
"   Harriet J. Page,
Dr. Moses H. Perkins, }
Mrs. Jane Perkins, {

Albert F. Preston. }
Mrs. Mary A. Preston, {

Leander Richardson. }
Mrs. Mary A. Richardson, {
Erving L. Richardson,
James H. Richardson. }
Mrs. Elizabeth T. Richardson, {
Elizur F. Reed. }
Mrs. Harriet A. Reed. {

Samuel Sawyer, }
Mrs. Amanda B. Sawyer, {
Clara E. Sawyer.

Mrs. Esther P. Tickner,
Sarah E. Tucker.

Lydia West.
George Wright. }
Mrs. Mersha M. Wright. {
Samuel F. West. }
Mrs. Charlotte P. West. }
Ashel O. Wright, }
Mrs. Lovisa Wright, {
Madison Woodward. }
Mrs. Harriet L. Woodward. {
George M. Woodward. }
Mrs. Emeline E. Woodward, {
Warren S. Worth. }
Mrs. Mary L. Worth. {
"   Jerusha C. Williams,
Emily C. Williams,
George A. Williams,
Mrs. Ellen M. Woodworth,
Mary N. West,
Emily A. Wright.

John S. Yeomans, }
Mrs. Sophia C. Yeomans. {
Frederick Yeomans, }
Mrs. Janette Yeomans, {
"   Seba Yeomans,
"   Harriet R. Yeomans,
Samuel D. Yeomans,
Sophia C. Yeomans,
L. Maria Yeomans.

CATALOGUE OF

MEMBERS OF THE ECCLESIASTICAL SOCIETY, COLUMBIA,

January 1, 1867.

Henry W. Buell,
Albert Brown,
William Collins,
Orren Clark,
Chester Clark,
Joseph Clark,
Lyman C. Clark,
Willard B. Clark,
Charles H. Clark,
Lorenzo W. Dewey,
Eleazer Dewey,
Elmore G. Dewey,
Silas H. Dewey,
Amasa B. Fuller,
Alanson H. Fuller,
Daniel T. Fuller,
Asher K. Fuller,
Charles R. Fuller,
George B. Fuller,
Simon Hunt,
Amasa A. Hunt,
Anson Holbrook,
Silas A. Holbrook,
Charles Holbrook,
John A. Hutchins,
Shubael S. Isham,

Benjamin Lyman,
Chester W. Lyman,
Alfred W. Lyman,
Samuel E. Lyman,
Henry E. Lyman,
William B. Little,
Giles Little,
Norman Little,
David D. Little,
James P. Little,
Horatio W. Little,
Samuel Little,
Norman P. Little,
George W. Morgan,
Albert F. Preston,
James H. Richardson,
Leander Richardson,
Samuel Sawyer,
Andrew P. Utley,
Samuel F. West,
Madison Woodward,
George Wright,
Asahel O. Wright,
George M. Woodward,
Samuel B. West,
John S. Yeomans.

THE FOLLOWING TABLE HAS BEEN FURNISHED BY REV.
MR. MOORE.

Year.	Mem.	Added by			Removed by			In. Bap.	Ben. Cont.
		Prof.	Let.	Tot'l.	Dth.	Dis.	Tot'l.		
1831	155	41	1	42	6	0	6	0	
1832	149	0	0	0	4	2	6	0	
1833	146	0	2	2	3	2	5	0	
1834	142	0	3	3	6	1	7	8	
1835	138	2	1	3	7	0	7	0	
1836	140	3	1	4	2	0	2	0	
1837	138	0	0	0	0	2	2	0	
1838	132	0	1	1	5	2	7	0	
1839	122	6	0	6	1	4	5	7	$153.03
1840	121	2	1	3	2	0	2	3	
1841	138	22	3	25	4	4	8	3	228.14
1842	136	6	1	7	5	2	7	8	198.02
1843	137	1	4	5	4	2	6	9	188.04
1844	132	1	0	1	5	2	7	5	200.54
1845	137	3	6	9	0	4	4	4	326.91 .
1846	136	0	4	4	3	2	5	5	
1847	137	0	3	3	2	0	2	2	
1848	133	0	3	3	5	2	7	3	
1849	120	0	0	0	4	3	7	3	
1850	118	0	4	4	1	4	5	3	
1851	120	7	1	8	3	3	6	4	138.65
1852	118	3	2	5	1	5	6	2	151.98
1853	116	1	2	3	5	0	5	6	146.70
1854	139	26	0	26	3	0	3	6	145.00
1855	139	0	2	2	2	0	2	12	125.68
1856	132	0	0	0	4	3	7	5	156.47
1857	130	0	1	1	3	0	3	6	135.87
1858	143	16	1	17	0	4	4	5	136.00
1859	140	1	0	1	3	1	4	2	142.00
1860	142	3	2	5	3	1	4	4	165.66
1861	135	0	0	0	7	0	7	3	115.94
1862	117	0	0	0	3	5	8	1	143.65
1863	114	0	2	2	3	3	6	2	143.34
1864	113	3	7	10	1	5	6	4	174.82
1865	132	22	0	22	1	2	3	3	209.82
1866	130	0	3	3	5	0	5	3	221.12
1867	169	36	3	39					

LETTER FROM REV. ASA D. SMITH, D. D., PRESIDENT OF
DARTMOUTH COLLEGE, NEW HAMPSHIRE.

DARTMOUTH COLLEGE, HANOVER, N. H., Oct. 22, 1866.

Rev. F. D. AVERY:

Dear Sir:

I very much regret that it will be out of my
power to be present at the approaching anniversary of your church.
Had I known of the occasion somewhat earlier, the case might have
been different; but as it is, engagements, which I cannot set aside,
will keep me here.

I feel the power of the associations to which you turn my thoughts.
A visit to the place where sprung into being Dartmouth College,
would be like tracing the source of some beautiful, fertilizing river to
its source among the distant mountains. It would give me a new
impression of the great issues which may come from small beginnings.
I should have a new impulse in my work, a fresh assurance that the
same good Providence which has guided this Institution from the
first, will make its future worthy of its noble past. I could add little
to the interest of the occasion, but I esteem it a loss to myself that I
cannot be with you.

Accept my thanks for the courtesy of your letter, and believe me,

Yours, very fraternally and truly,

ASA D. SMITH.

————

LETTER FROM GOVERNOR BUCKINGHAM.

NORWICH, CONN., Oct. 19, 1866.

Rev. F. D. AVERY, Columbia:

My Dear Sir:

I thank you for your invitation to be pres-
ent at the celebration of the 150th Anniversary of your church, and
should accept the same, if I had not an engagement which will detain
me nearly all of next week in New York. I assure you that I feel
a deep interest in all that pertains to the history and prosperity of
Lebanon, in its former boundaries, and in all her churches. The
good seed which has been sown for a century and a half has produced

a valuable harvest in your immediate vicinity; but I doubt not that the fruit which is unseen, and that which has matured in other parts of our country, is vastly richer than that which is seen.

With high regard,

I am your obedient servant,

WM. A. BUCKINGHAM.

LETTER FROM REV. DANIEL HUNT, POMFRET, CONN.

Rev. F. D. Avery:

Dear Brother:

I return my hearty thanks to you and the committee for your invitation to attend the approaching anniversary of the formation of the church and society in Columbia. It would afford me great pleasure to be present on the occasion, which I trust will be one of great interest and satisfaction to all the sons and daughters of that ancient precinct of Lebanon, "The Crank." The early history of the place was honorable. Distinguished men dwelt there. Shining characters were born and reared there, and went forth to bless the world by their labors. And God has never forgotten his church in that place, though it has often been in great affliction and peril. Zion stands and rejoices there still, and the spirit of Wheelock and Brockway lingers within the gates, which is always a comfort for me to think of.

It is not likely that I can be present on the occasion; or if such a thing should be, it would not be well for you to depend on me for any service; for I am nothing now, and, as you know, "ex nihilo nihil fit."

Yours truly,

D. HUNT.

Pomfret, July 18, 1866

NOTE A.

LETTER OF THE PARISH TO REV. E. WHEELOCK, D. D., RELATING TO THE LOCATION OF THE CHARITY SCHOOL.

"At a legal and full meeting of the Inhabitants, legal voters of the second society in Lebanon, [Now Columbia,] in Connecticut, held in said society on the 29th day of June, Anno Domini 1767, We made choice of Mr. James Pinneo to be moderator of said meeting, and passed the following votes, *nemine contradicente.*

1. That we desire the Indian Charity School now under the care of the Rev. Mr. Eleazer Wheelock, may be fixed to continue in this society; provided it may consist with the interest and prosperity of said School.

2. That as we have a large and convenient house for public and divine Worship; we will accommodate the members of said school with such convenient seats in said house as we shall be able.

3. That the following letter be presented to the Rev. Mr. Eleazer Wheelock, by Messrs. Israel Woodward, James Pinneo, and Asahel Clark, in the name and behalf of this society; and that they desire him to transmit a copy of the same, with the votes foregoing, to the Right Honorable the Earl of Dartmouth, and the rest of those Honorable and Worthy Gentlemen in England who have condescended to patronize said school; and to whom the establishment of the same is committed.

The Inhabitants of the second society in Lebanon in Connecticut to the Rev. Mr. Eleazer Wheelock, Pastor of said society.

Rev. and dear Pastor,

As you are witness to our past care and concern for the success of your most pious and charitable undertaking in favor of the poor perishing Indians on this continent, we are confident you will not be displeased at our addressing you on this occasion; but that you would rather think it strange if we should altogether hold our peace at such a time as this; when we understand it is still in doubt both with your self and Friends where to fix your school; whether at Albany or more remote among the Indian Tribes, in this society where it was first planted, or in some other part of this colony proposed for its accommodation.

We have some of us heard most of the arguments offered for its removal, and however plausable they appear we are not at all convinced of their force, or that it is expedient, every thing considered, it should be removed, nor do we think we have great reason to fear the event, only we would not be wanting as to our duty in giving such hints in favor of its continuance here as naturally occur to our minds, for we have that confidence in you and the friends of the desire, that you will not be easily carried away with Appearances: but will critically observe the secret springs of those generous offers, made in one place and another, (some of which are beyond what we can pretend to,) whether some prospect of private emolument be not at the bottom; or whether they will finally prove more kind to your pious institution as such considered, (whatever their pretenses may be,) than ever have been or at present appear to be to the Redeemer's Kingdom in general. We trust this institution so well calculated to the advancement of its interest will flourish best among the Redeemer's friends; and although with respect to ourselves we have little to boast as to friendship to our divine Redeemer or his interest, yet this we are sure of, that he has been very kind to us, in times past, and we trust has made you the instrument of much good to us, and to lay a foundation for it to succeeding generations; we humbly hope God has been preparing an habitation for himself here, and has said of it this is my resting place, here will I dwell forever, (not because they deserved it,) but because I have desired it, and where God is pleased to dwell, under his influence your institution (which we trust is of him,) may Expect to live and thrive. We desire it may be considered that this is its birth place, here it was kindly received, and nourished when no other door was set open to it—here it found friends when almost friendless, yea when despised and contemned abroad—its friends are now increased here as well as elsewhere, and although by reason of our poverty and the hardness of the times, our subscriptions are small compared with what some others may boast. Being at present but about (£)810 pounds lawful money yet there are here some other privileges which we think very valuable and serviceable to the design, viz. 400 acres of very fertile and good land, about forty acres of which are under improvement, and the remainder well set with choice timber and fuel, and is suitably proportioned for the various branches of Husbandry which will much accommodate the design as said land is situated within about half a mile of our Meeting House, and may be purchased for fifty shillings lawful money per acre. There is also several other small parcels of land suitably situate for building places for the use of the school to be sold at a reasonable rate. We have also a beautiful building place for said school within a few rods of said meeting house,

12

adjacent to which is a large and pleasant Green : and we are confident that wood, provisions and clothing, &c., which will be necessary for the school, may be had here not only now, but in future years at as low a rate as in any place in the colony, or in any other place where it has been proposed to settle your school. These privileges we think are valuable and worthy your consideration, and also of those Honourable and worthy Gentlemen in England to whom you have committed the design of the affair, and from the friendly disposition which has so many years past and does still reign in our breasts towards it. We think it may be presumed we shall from time to time be ready to minister to its support as occasion shall require and our circumstances permit. We take the liberty further to observe that such has hitherto been the peace and good order (greatly through your instrumentality,) obtaining among us that the members of your school have all along been as free from temptations to any vicious courses or danger of fatal error as perhaps might be expected they would be on any spot of this Universally polluted Globe.

Here, Dear Sir, your school has flourished remarkably. It has grown apace; from small beginnings how very considerable it has become; an evidence that the soil and climate suit the institution—if you transplant it you run a risk of stinting its growth, perhaps of destroying its very life, or at least of changing its nature and missing the pious aim you have all along had in view; a danger which scarce need to be hinted; as you are sensible it has been the common fate of institutions of this kind; that charitable Donations have been misapplied and perverted to serve purposes very far from or contrary to those the pious donors had in view; such is the subtilty of the old serpent that he will turn all our weapons against our selves if possible. Aware of this, you have all along appeared to decline and even detest all such alliances and proposals as were calculated for, or seemed to promise any private emolument to your self or your friends. This we trust is still your prevailing temper and rejoice to hear that your friends and those who are intrusted with the affair in England are exactly in the same sentiments, happy presage not only of the continuance of the institution itself but we hope of its immutability as to place. One thing more we beg leave to mention, (not to tire your patience with the many that occur,) viz. if you remove the school from us, you at the same time take away our Minister, the light of our eyes and joy of our hearts, under whose ministrations we have sat with great delight; whose labors have been so acceptable and we trust profitable for a long time; must then our Dear and Worthy Pastor and his pious institution go from us together? Alas shall we be deprived of both in one day? We are sensible that we have abused such privileges and have forfeited them; and at God's bar we plead guilty—we pray him to give us repentance and reformation, and to lengthen out our Happy State; we own the justice of God in so heavy losses, if they must be inflicted; and even in the removal of our Candlestick out of its place, but we can't bear the thought that you our Dear Pastor and the dear friends to your pious institution should become the Executioners of such a Vengeance. However we leave the matter with you, and are with much Duty and filial regard Dear Sir, Your very humble servants or rather Obedient Children.

By order of said Society,
       { ISRAEL WOODWARD,
       JAMES PINNEO,
       ASAHEL CLARK, JR.

June 29th, 1767.

NOTE B.*

LETTER RECOMMENDING REV. MR. WHITAKER IN HIS EFFORTS SOLICITING SUBSCRIPTIONS FOR MOOR'S CHARITY SCHOOL.

Mr. Whitaker was a man of fine talents and prepossessing appearance. He had manifested great interest in the prosperity of Mr. Wheelock's Indian School at Lebanon, and in the welfare of the Mohegan Indians, his neighbors. On these accounts he had been selected as a proper person to accompany Mr. Occom on his mission.

They carried with them a printed book containing recommendations, and an exposition of the state of Indian Missions in North America. Mr. Whitaker's recommendation from his church is as follows:

The Church of Christ at Chelsey, in Norwich, in Conn: in New England, to all the Churches of Christ, and whomsoever it may concern, send greeting:

Whereas it has pleased God in his Providence, to call our Reverend and worthy Pastor, Mr. Nathaniel Whitaker, from us for a season, to go to Europe, to solicit charities for the Indian Charity School, under the care of the Rev. Mr. Eleazer Wheelock, of Lebanon, and to promote Christian Knowledge among the Indians on this continent:

* By permission from "Caulkins' History of Norwich."

We do unanimously recommend him, the said Mr. Whitaker and his services to all the Churches and people of God, of whatever denomination, and wheresoever he may come, as a faithful minister of Jesus Christ, whose praise is in the gospel through the churches; earnestly requesting brotherly kindness and charity may be extended towards him as occasion may require; and that the grand and important cause in which he is engaged, may be forwarded and promoted by all the lovers of truth.

Wishing grace, mercy and truth may be multiplied to you and the whole Israel of God, and desiring an interest in your prayers, we subscribe   Yours in the faith and fellowship of the gospel,

By order and in behalf)   JONATHAN HUNTINGTON,
   said Church,   )   ISIAH TIFFANY.
Norwich, Oct. 21st, 1766.

The delegates were eminently successful in their mission, both in England and Scotland, and collected funds amounting nearly to ten thousand pounds sterling.

The following letter, written by Occom from London to his daughters at home, is a curious example of Mohegan ingenuity:

My dear Mary and Esther—

Perhaps you may query whether I am well: I came from home well, was by the way well, got over well, am received at London well, and am treated extremely well,—yea, I am caress'd too well. And do you pray that I may be well; and that I may do well, and in Time return Home well. And I hope you are well, and wish you well, and as I think you begun well, so keep on well, that you may end well, and then all will be well.

And so Farewell,

Samson Occom

www.ingramcontent.com/pod-product-compliance
Lightning Source LLC
Chambersburg PA
CBHW021409090426
42742CB00009B/1068